FACING THE CENTER

FACING THE CENTER

*Toward an Identity Politics of
One-to-One Mentoring*

HARRY C. DENNY

UTAH STATE UNIVERSITY PRESS
Logan, Utah
2010

Utah State University Press
Logan, Utah 84322-7800

Manufactured in the United States of America
Cover design by Barbara Yale-Read

Library of Congress Cataloging-in-Publication Data

Denny, Harry C.
  Facing the center : toward an identity politics of one-to-one mentoring / Harry C. Denny/.
    p. cm.
  Includes bibliographical references and index.
  ISBN 978-0-87421-767-4 (pbk.) -- ISBN 978-0-87421-768-1 (e-book)
  1. English language--Rhetoric--Study and teaching. 2. Report writing--Study and teaching
(Higher) 3. Writing centers--Political aspects. 4. Mentoring. 5. Multicultural education. I. Title.

  PE1404.D3887 2010
  808'.0420711--dc22

                          2009047228

To
COURTNEY *&* MAX
my companions in life and writing.

CONTENTS

ACKNOWLEDGMENTS

This book would not have been possible without the generous funding from St. John's University's summer research grant program that I received for Summer 2008 and 2009 and the regular ongoing assistance that institution provides. The summer funding made possible time to focus and produce and reflects the investment in faculty research that Provost Julie Upton, St. John's College of Arts & Sciences Dean Jeffrey Fagan, and Associate Dean for Staten Island Kelly Rocca, each have historically made. My English department Chair, Steve Sicari, and the Director of St. John's Institute for Writing Studies, Derek Owens, have not only been strong and encouraging leaders and advocates of this project; they have also acted as two of the best mentors a junior faculty member can wish for.

In the writing centers, the associate directors, Tom Philipose and Chris Leary, have provided sound leadership and unwavering support, especially when I've needed to close my door or disappear to write for blocks of time. Without all that they do, the quality and speed with which I produced this manuscript wouldn't have happened. Besides these fine men, my support staff is both generous and protective. Connie DeSimone at Staten Island and Virginia Buccino at Queens acted as the best buffers and protectors I could ask for, and just as important, they were both touchstones who grounded me and empathized always at just the right moments. Connie, in particular, made driving over the Verrazano Bridge week in, week out, worth every toll because of the pure positive energy and drive with which she infuses everything. More so than most, she kept me moving and enthusiastic. Dorothy Bukay, the staff assistant for the larger Institute in Queens, has always been a rock and a trusted resource, and I thank her for her support as well.

This book grew out of a conference presentation at the 2007 Conference on College Composition and Communication in New York City. The panel, "(Un)Covering Identities: Theorizing the Construction, Resistance, and Interplay of Minority Identities in a Majority Academy and World," included Courtney Frederick, Rochell Issac, Anna Rita

Napoleone, and Elizabeth Weaver. We all still plan an edited collection that explores the dynamics of "covering" in a variety of teaching contexts.

Thomas Ferrell and Moira Ozias were valued peers who helped me workshop and hone early chapter drafts when I spent a month at the University of Kansas doing an intensive writing retreat. Anna Rita Napoleone, Anne Ellen Geller, Pat Belanoff, Michele Eodice, Kami Day and Frankie Condon spurred along drafting and revising, whether they posted comments, talked me through revisions and texts to complicate my thinking, or became voices in my head which whom I could dialogue. Lauren Kopec, a doctoral student in English, worked with me to develop the index and voiced needed encouragement throughout the waning days of this book's production.

As the manuscript entered the final stages, Michael Spooner and the anonymous reviewers couldn't have offered better, more challenging, affirming guidance for improving what this text ultimately became. Quite often during the process, I doubted whether this book was possible or that it would even matter. Along with all the people above, I can't imagine someone more suited to mentor and guide a writer like me who doubts as much as he believes than Michael.

This book has been a labor, a journey with peaks and valleys, moments when it didn't seem like it'd ever come to closure, times when it created deep elation and frustration. Nobody else experienced and tolerated all that was involved, and nobody else has more fingerprints on this project and lingering influence than Courtney Frederick. While this book imagines many interlocutors, he is among the most important. My talks with him, his sacrificed time, and his patience to read and reassure kept me going these last couple of years. I hope everyone, just once in life, has the luck to have a soul mate and intellectual companion sharing the same home; with Courtney, it made all the work vibrant and meaningful because he understands and cares as much as I do about the power and potential for spaces like writing centers where people come to collaborate and grow with one another.

naïve tutor has an epiphany that cross-pollinates, spurring on and bettering the wider crew. Such narratives have an archive in the *Writing Lab Newsletter*, the monthly publication whose volumes provide a rich education in writing center thought and practice. I might share tutoring and tutor-training case studies that reinforce what we already know works well. The pages of *Landmark Essays*, research monographs, essays in *Writing Center Journal* and the postings on WCenter, the field's digital clearinghouse and support kiosk, well document the field's collective wisdom. Points of comparison for pay rates, staffing levels, and institution positioning can be found at the Writing Centers Research Project. Any of this work—what-to-do sorts of questions—operates on the assumption, on some level, that writing centers can just bank and replicate without regard to local context or culture or without deep thinking in collaboration with a staff and other stakeholders—faculty, students, and administrators. Granted, research in composition and writing center studies offers crucial guidance, benchmarks and best practices, none of them of much utility outside the everyday realities of our sites and experiences, whether they are emergent, established or senior. The writers of *The Everyday Writing Center* are the most recent to address and reinforce those sorts of insights (Geller et al. 2007).

I want to tell another tale, a set of tales in fact, rooted in a phenomenon that cuts across writing centers, that resists easy answers and offers up tough questions, that invites problem-posing and believing and doubting. Typically when the issue of "face" is addressed, people pose it is as a sort of rhetorical sort of problem: "How do we put the best face forward?" "What's the best face to put on this issue?" "Let's face the facts." "Putting a face on…" This book posits face as a starting point for inquiry, asking us to think about it in multiple ways, and pushing us to bracket quick recipes for resolution. *Facing the Center* is about process and politics and their implications for learning and teaching, particularly in the context of one-to-one collaborations. At its core, face is about identity and raises questions about who we are, and how we come to know and present identity, as a phenomenon that's unified, coherent, and captured in a singular essence, or as something more multi-faceted and dynamic. While on one level, I want us to think about face vis-à-vis writing centers; I also want us to be aware of margins and center, to think of the ways of privileging, to explore the dynamics of ordinary caste. Put simply, as much as I hope for us to grapple with the identities that circulate through writing centers and tutoring,

I also want us to think about the transparency of identity, where bodies and affects seem to exist and perform *beyond* or *post* identity, where they seem the "same" or "other." Facing the center requires an awareness that the identities at the center signify just as richly as those at the margin. In the move to foreground identity, I commit to the principle that the center, like the margin, has a face and needs interrogation and mapping. In an ever-globalizing world where corporate America and colleges and universities race to embrace and champion diversity, it remains illusive because Others often don't seem present, but a face and a center are nonetheless generative.[1]

St. John's students embody that very diversity most colleges strive for and their viewbooks often trumpet. Intercultural contact, learning, and teaching are part of the ether on campus, augmented no doubt by being situated at the crossroads of New York City. In that very characteristic face that's uncommon in other places around the country, St. John's students are also very typical. They think of college as the route to vocation and job security, undergraduate learning as a conduit to graduate training, professional curricula as entrée and apprenticeship in specialized discourse communities. What drives students is quite similar from campus to campus whether they live in Jamaica, Queens; Bensonhurst, Brooklyn; or in Madison, Amherst, or Eugene. But attending to diversity isn't axiomatic to urban colleges; the relative homogeneity of higher education beyond city centers begs for just as much consideration, not just to prepare students for life in a global village, but also to help students contest the hegemonic as arbitrary and provisional. As I've moved around the U.S. and visited a wide range of writing centers and the professionals who staff them, I've been struck by the need to account for not so much the pragmatics of what we do, but the bodies and the politics that accompany them in writing centers.

Wherever I've gone in the U.S., I've seen writing centers staffed with people in generally privileged positions working with clients who were more often than not first-generation, working-class, or non-traditional students, as likely to be people of color as white. I've seen writing center directors situated as Others by virtue of institutional position or

---

1.   My capitalization of the term "Other," reflects a conventional usage in sociology, cultural studies, and the wider humanities and social sciences. It is a cover term for the wider group of marginalized people, those who are variously understood as outside the mainstream, and Other represents an identity around which people mobilize into formal social and identity movements as well as loosely-organized networks of mutual recognition and support.

academic rank more marginal than the student demographic they were ostensibly reaching out to. I would discover administrators making do in writing centers, thwarted from pursuing passions in some other field, biding their time and marginally, minimally investing in their unit's programming and development. From coast to coast, I've seen elite universities create writing centers to, as Nancy Grimm (1999) argues, absolve themselves of any further responsibility to "at-risk" students, typically coded as Others, or of any sense of social obligation to the communities in which they were situated. More often than not, in writing center after writing center, in hushed whispers or flustered outbursts, conversations would edge toward the Others in their midst, from the vulgar, "Why does this school let them in if they can't handle it?" to the more subtle discourses grounded in static notions of argumentation or academic or standard English. Veiled at every turn—whether the object of concern was a center's staffing, its clients, administration, mission, philosophy, structure or processes—were bodies in the center, bodies with identities, bodies with faces, politics and implications. With rare exception, nobody was talking about them, a collective denial no doubt rooted more in inability than refusal.[2] This ambivalence about facing the center suggests a discomfort with complexity, with attention to the intersection of meta-forces and local influences at play in writing centers.

That epiphany—that identity politics are real and uncharted in writing centers—first struck me years ago when I began working in writing centers during graduate school. Sadly, the pattern has held up over the years as I moved from one academic post to another. Early on in my career, I stumbled into a community in writing centers, complete with informal networks of colleagues, regional conferences, special interest groups, and national organizations. This world has unparalleled collegiality in the academy; mutual support and mentoring is never more than a telephone call, email posting, or conference cocktail drink away. But it's a community not without problems, both ones it names and analyzes and ones that go unexamined and neglected. Some bemoan writing centers' standing in academe and strive to elevate them by

2.   Among the exceptions are the important dialogue on anti-racism that Victor Villaneueva (2003, 2006) and Frankie Condon (2007) have fostered as well as the ongoing special interest group work Moira Ozias, Beth Godbee and others have been conducting at national and regional conferences in composition and writing center studies.

privileging scholarship (be it critical, empirical or qualitative), championing quality service to students, or fostering socially-conscious outreach. Others are critical of the execution of writing centers and question staffing by people not rooted in the field's professional literature, by individuals whose primary focus isn't administering their units, or by folks who don't (or can't) command sufficient support from their institutions. Just as composition studies claims a good deal of victimhood by being positioned (or positioning itself) as a step-child in larger English Studies and literary scholarship, writing center academics can follow a similar path, viewing the field as further subsidiary, narrowly restricted to the pragmatics of day-to-day (or session-to-session) execution of practice. But that's a tired reading of our position that makes us passive objects of our fates, instead of active leaders working toward other directions, other possibilities. To riff on Richard Miller's 2005 work, writing center studies, like wider English Studies, risks going the way of the Classics if we don't play an active role in making our field and the humanities relevant and vital to a post-industrial academy. Part of that work requires asking a different, perhaps difficult, set of questions about who and what we represent as a discipline. Interrogating our identity and its operation involves addressing more than the structural exclusion of certain voices and the institutional privileging or normalizing of others. The causal roots and solutions to those issues are simultaneously internal to writing centers and external to the macrodynamics of higher education, particularly with respect to access and social and cultural honoring of the humanities as a profession.

For the wider writing center community, the absence of experiences and voices of Others has been conspicuous, but also jarring. It isn't as though people of color, working-class folks and non-native speakers of English aren't often part of the conversations or considered in debates; more often than not, these groups are the objects of inquiry. Even more curious, participants themselves seem unaware of their own constructed identities, privileged or Other, center or marginal. Talks, presentations, and keynotes index Others as objects for whom practical and instrumental learning applies, not figures for whom learning is necessarily transactional and collaborative ("we" can learn from "them," "they" from "us.").

As conferences and meetings blurred from one to another, I became aware of a collective dissonance between writing center personnel and the people with whom they worked. It was as if no material connections existed between populations: "they" turn to "us" to become better "writers" as if "we" hadn't ourselves, regardless of circumstances, ever journeyed (or continue to journey) toward claiming "writer" as part of our ensemble of identities. Or further, "we" assume "they" don't have literacies perfectly rich and productive or have rhetorical traditions and cultures of expression that are impossible to bridge or mesh. Or better, "we" act on the flawed assumption or sense of being that "we" have authentic selves or essences that aren't themselves subject to a politics of status or history of caste. Simply, too many risk the delusion that their bodies are not marked or over-determined by identities. Underrepresented, at best, or invisible, at worst, have been the professionals and clients at high schools, two-year colleges, and historically Black or Hispanic-serving colleges and universities, all of which are institutional sites which, if included, reached out to, heard and listened to, promise to radically re-imagine what the "community" of writing centers has to offer, assuming they have the capacity to index, name, and reflect on identities themselves. Still, my privileged colleagues—white, middle-class, straight, American—would ponder why "they" (the Others) weren't more present, more a part of "us," though we rarely embraced them or reflected on our own complicity in silencing and failing to listen to them.

These tensions and challenges aren't unique to writing centers, and they are also not endemic to them. This book will argue, instead, writing centers are sites *par excellance* where these issues are worked through in ways that wider composition studies and teaching across the disciplines can learn from. Writing centers make local, material and individual all the larger forces at play that confound, impede, and make possible education in institutions. Digging deep into these dynamics and reimaging our theories and practices based on such labor isn't the exclusive province of writing centers; the wider academy must also take up this work and consider ways to follow the lead of writing centers or to clear new ground unique to individual institutional or program/ disciplinary contexts. To face the center isn't just about knowing the who and appreciating the complexity of identities, both marginal and privileged; it's also about the politics of our process, *how* we face and to what impact. That journey, for me and this text, begins with recounting my own discovery and coming to terms with identity and activism. I write about the influence of identity movements, both historical ones and those I've been involved with, on me and on my later work as a professional in writing centers. Among the lessons that I'll share is the importance of attending to identity politics and the tangible effects of political, economic, social, and cultural forces at play in and often confounding education wherever it's practiced.

MAPPING SELF, MAPPING IDENTITY

All this discussion of identity suggests I somehow possess a keen sensitivity and intuitiveness about the complexity and practices of subject positions and their performance. It begs the question of the roots to my own (ongoing) self-awareness of identity as well as motives for the circumspection. My own discovery of identity and its politics began when I was an undergraduate at the University of Iowa, where a community of interdisciplinary scholars taught me critical, social, and cultural theory. This learning under the auspices of an American Studies department happened just as I was exploring and calling into question my sense of self and its possibilities. These professors taught me about the history of class struggle, the origins of patriarchy, and the foundations of critical race studies, and the early debates around what would be called queer theory. As wars on political correctness waged throughout academe, about what some thought was a dubious pedagogy of empowerment and critical voice sweeping many classrooms, I was unwittingly having my consciousness raised. A new language and ways of thinking were turning me into a new kind of activist, not one who touted placards or bumper stickers, not one who would march on offices, but one who would discover everyday teaching and learning moments led to change every bit as important and sustainable as the more dramatic forms of protest in the streets or speeches from podiums. During those undergraduate years, I was discovering my own identity as a working-class person, as a queer, as someone who never viewed the world without being attuned to the lenses that constituted my ability to see. I would not have a self-awareness of this intellectual growth and change in me until much, much later in life when I moved from advocating for change in often abstract terms, removed from local tangibility. In writing centers, I would finally learn that consciousness-raising, advocating self-empowerment and fostering critical awareness of social, cultural, economic, and political forces on institutions, communities and individuals, might reap rewards in ways material and beyond. I came to realize identity wasn't merely about self-discovery; I also began to understand its rhetorical dimensions, that how identity was invoked (its presentation) mattered and that, when well-executed, could make social change happen, maybe not monumental change, but local shifts or micro-successes, that might culminate in a tipping point.

This nexus of the politics of identity with an attention to its audience impact, what might be termed its dynamics of face, would reassert itself over and over again. At St. John's and the other schools where I've taught, the face of the writing centers was often their most striking element. These spaces provided complex nodal points where students, tutors, staff, faculty, and administrators alike met wider institutional, and consequently larger, social, cultural, economic and political forces. How well this or that writing center works with all those that circulate through it isn't merely an index of how on task or effective we are with the fundamentals of teaching, mentoring and learning. The efficacy of the contemporary writing center is also predicated on the degree to which it problem-poses the everyday in relation to the meta-currents circulating about it. What has made me most proud of St. John's, then, isn't just the instrumentality of what we do; rather, our successes and failures also happen in relation to the faces this unit represents and empowers as well as the degree to which we reflect upon the politics and material consequences imbedded in them. Still I wonder, in the midst of all this diversity, what is not being interrogated. I think of Royster's (1996) caution about the politics of silence, of what goes unsaid, or Condon's (2007) call to question the structural, institutional, and individual roots of oppression and the ways our pedagogies reinforce and make them visible.

Identity is ubiquitous to the everyday life of writing centers. For them, struggles with face involve a complicated juggling of identities in relation to perceived audiences. A consultant calls me aside and shares an experience with racism that peers would dismiss as hypersensitivity. Other tutors tell me of students' sexual advances, and another group speaks about gendered differences in students' and consultants' approaches to tutoring. Colleagues and students alike confide embarrassment at people's reactions to their accented English. In a tutoring pedagogy course, a student comes out to me after reading some of my earlier work. I comfort students, native and non-native English speakers, stung by feedback from professors who banish them to the writing center or insult their literacy ("You can't write!"), students who easily figure out that the common denominator in such comments is their identity position as Other. The politics of those moments have everything to do with who people are and how they perform and present their identities. Very little scholarship from writing center or composition studies, beyond literacy narratives made famous by Mike Rose (2005), Richard Rodriquez (1983), Victor Villanueva (1993), Min Zhan Lu (1994), bell hooks (1994), and others, offers guidance when the politics of identity cuts through both the process and product of writing and mentoring writers. This book will not offer a comprehensive catalog of recipes for handling those and other still unanticipated eruptions of identity politics in writing center conferences. Instead, this book will unpack those moments, working to theorize what makes them possible as well as their implications.

When I experience identity politics in the writing center, I make sense of those moments and their implications from other chapters of my life, where the gnawing lessons of oppression in the U.S. came to me through experience, conversation and study. These experiences and their implications usually exceed the pragmatics of action–of prescriptions for what to do when; rather, identity movements and the politics that they taught me testified to the importance and centrality of struggles over meaning and their consequences for citizenship, learning and teaching. Identity movements, composition studies and writing centers are inexorably tied to one another by history and necessity, but weaving them together hasn't been charted before. These lessons push conventional debates in the field toward a critical study of the politics of identity and facing the center. At the same time, one's own experience is just that: one's own experience. Those very lenses that provide us with subject positions and vantages from which to view the world are limiting and flawed to the extent that they are taken as totalizing, not as starting points and spaces for questions and reflection, especially from the perspective of someone else.

THE LIMITS OF "STREET" ACTIVISM

My discovery of and involvement with identity movements centered on civil rights work in Colorado and HIV/AIDS activism in Philadelphia. The lessons learned as an organizer and protester would frustrate me ultimately, but they would enable me to imagine writing center work in ways that could contribute to change in local, sustainable ways. The Colorado experience revolved around Amendment 2, a referendum that banned civil rights on the basis of sexual identity, and my work with the Equal Protection Campaign (EPOC), the grassroots group challenging the initiative and its main supporter, Colorado for Family Values. My role in EPOC was as a participant in a steering committee charged with reaching out to communities of color and soliciting their organizations' involvement and support opposing Amendment 2. As we moved from groups like the NAACP to La Raza and spoke to one community leader after another, we discovered division, tension and suspicion directed toward the gay community. Mobilizing against the referendum required us to reach beyond self-interest and to understand the measure in a wider context of historical assaults on civil rights in Colorado and beyond, moves the community not only wasn't prepared to make, but hadn't even conceived of doing. I discovered the organized gay community had done little to combat earlier civil rights challenges, from anti-immigrant sentiment to English-only legislation and anti-affirmative action lawsuits. With a political climate already rife with hostility toward Others, I learned that many on the left and in the civil rights movement thought implicitly, "Where were you people when...?" My committee didn't have answers, and we represented a community who hadn't expressed outrage when Spanish-speaking Latinos were stigmatized, when people of color in general were marginalized and viewed with suspicion, when poor people's humanity was called into question. In the wake of decades-long rollbacks of already weakly supported Great Society programs once meant to foster empowerment and social justice, I discovered little energy among people who might otherwise be natural allies to challenge what turned out to be a popularity contest about homosexuality and gay rights, especially when queer people had been largely silent in earlier campaigns just as offensive and hurtful to the symbolic and material status of other marginal people in Colorado. Amendment 2 succeeded and my community failed because we couldn't see or combat the seeds of social and cultural intolerance sown years earlier.

Leaders representing the African American and Latino communities were conflicted, and understandably so. They were smart and politically astute and recognized the threat of anti-gay legislation, but they also saw the handwriting on the wall. Amendment 2 was going to pass (and it did), and it was going to pass in part because it was framed as a popularity contest about queer people (who weren't popular), but also a vote on civil rights (which weren't either). Civil rights were being cast as having overreached, having begun to threaten on some level the privilege held by whites, men, and the middle-class. Conventional civil rights activists were reluctant to leverage their tenuous successes for another set of claimants, especially when many of those claimants possessed financial and political resources that would have been helpful earlier, in other battles. Even more, considering the oppression that sexual minorities experienced on a host of fronts (employment, healthcare, housing, etc.), the face of the movement was disproportionately privileged and used the mantra of civil rights as a platform for wider social acceptance and legitimacy, not as a remedy for past wrongs. Long-time civil rights activists, particularly those active from the 1950s to early 1970s, were also justifiably offended at the prospect of white, middle-class gay men and lesbians evoking the language and imagery of the wider movement without having struggled or having been participants themselves. These latter-day gay civil rights activists were relatively young, held no ties to the New Left activism, and didn't reach out, honor, or coalesce with those who spoke from experiences that complicated sexual identity and whose identity intersected with forms of oppression that possessed different roots and histories. That inability for the gay community to see its struggles as tied to those of others (and theirs to its) was confounded by the reality of a community conflicted about itself. How did it understand identity? What was its history and relationship to other forms of identity? What were the connections between individual and community when it came to identity?

When doctoral study drew me to Philadelphia, I found myself writing a dissertation about those very dynamics and unexplored questions around Amendment 2 and re-discovering activism around AIDS that I had participated in and studied years before back in Iowa. In the mid-1980s, I came of age as a young gay man in a world dominated by HIV. Those early years of that health crisis were the stuff of folklore: breathless new media coverage, vertiginous public policy debates, communities reeling. It was a time where sex and sexuality seemed toxic, where illness circulated as much as a metaphor of morality as an index of immunological complexity. Since so much of the past thirty years of AIDS in America has been constructed as an issue owned by its urban centers, Iowa might seem like an odd incubator for activism—AIDS, queer or otherwise. As the threat of AIDS was emerging, economic recession decimated family farms and laid waste to unionized manufacturing and meatpacking jobs.[3] These dawning days of the

---

3.   For more background on the 1980s farm crisis, read Harl's *Farm Debt Crisis of the 1980s* (1990), Dudley's *Debt & Dispossession: Farm Loss in America's Heartland* (2000),

Rust Belt created a political bouillabaisse imbued with radicalism; suspicion of industry, government, and change; populism and provincialism. Prairie Fire coexisted with a resurgence of Klan organizing, violent union clashes commingled with stoic acquiescence to economic reality. Very few people actually lived Iowa's storied farm culture, but the struggle to survive in a world of ever-shifting socio-economic rules generated, for some, a strong working-class identity that cut across blue-collar vocations and bound many together. Losing a multi-generation family farm operation was no less bitter than watching a centuries-old meatpacking plant clang its rusty gates shut one last time, its rancid smell now only a romantic memory of legions who had passed before. That was the world I grew up in.

When AIDS hit my college town, Iowa City, it swept through the gay male community. One after another, my role models seroconverted, many dying in those early years and still others going on to live and teach the rest how to cope with dignity and agency. With the town's summer stock and literary connections to New York City and Chicago, Iowa City was an urban outpost experiencing AIDS, only on a smaller scale. People living with AIDS came back to reconnect and hospice with families, and parents and siblings who were, by day, farm-hands or factory workers and suddenly became ad hoc caregivers and community educators. Early on, the queer community mobilized around the crisis with formal and ad hoc social networks to support, advocate, research, and educate, even as the national media framed AIDS as urban/racialized and gay/sexualized.[4] In Rock Hudson, Ryan White, Freddie Mercury, Africa, and Magic Johnson, the media discovered and re-discovered the crisis (Denny 1997a, 1997b). Coverage would intone a sympathetic yet patronizing desire to put a "human face on AIDS," but implying earlier faces of AIDS had been somehow less than human.

At the time, I was little more than a spectator on the sidelines as friends tried to mimic protests by local "chapters" of ACT UP!, the New York City-originated grassroots activist group that launched dramatic, media-savvy actions against governmental and pharmaceutical responses to HIV through the late-1980s and early 1990s. When I

Gray-Davidson's *Broken Heartland: The Rise of America's Rural Ghetto* (1996), and Fitchen's *Endangered Spaces, Enduring Places: Change, Identity, and Survival in Rural America* (1991).

4.   For more on the social and cultural history of AIDS, see Patton (1985, 1990, 1998, 2002), and Epstein (1998).

got to Philly I was burned out from Amendment 2 and wanted to do a different sort of activism. Being in a city with a large organized gay community, I thought I could finally put my study—I'd even done a Master's thesis on media representation of people with AIDS—into some sort of action. I turned to ACT UP!. By this time, the group's agenda had moved beyond pushing local, state and federal governments, as well as the pharmaceutical industry, to be more responsive to the broader populations dealing with the epidemic. ACT UP! was advocating for better healthcare access and more progressive policy toward risk reduction, more specifically trying to get the federal government to fund or at least not sanction local efforts to reach injecting drug users. The group and other allied, non-governmental agencies had launched education campaigns directed at helping I.V. drug users reduce their risk for HIV and other illnesses by cleaning "works" or exchanging contaminated needles for safe ones. Although the guerilla education was reducing infection rates, the Clinton administration wouldn't fund such projects because it feared conservative backlash for being soft on drug enforcement. Instead, it continued the War-on-Drugs, "Just Say No!" policies of abstinence and policing drug use begun under the earlier Reagan and Bush administrations; this face of AIDS, unlike other more mainstream ones, didn't have caché with the wider public and couldn't draw upon a reservoir of compassion or empathy. People without access to healthcare or addicted to injecting drugs still drew scorn, making inattention or harassment more politically expedient than changing attitudes and policy.

From my earlier experiences with civil rights activism to this work on AIDS, I learned a good deal about the limits and possibilities of contemporary identity movements and their implications for making change. One important lesson involved honoring historical intersections of social, cultural, economic, and political forces in the context where the need for action arises. For AIDS, it meant understanding that the illness was never just about a virus or set of opportunistic infections; rather, to riff on Susan Sontag's (1990, 1989) famous line, AIDS was always already a metaphor, a culmination of social and cultural values about sexuality, race, gender, class, nationality, healthcare, and more. What confounded government and industry was the realization that activists wouldn't ignore those currents (e.g., that there was a long-established history of pathologizing sexual minorities and people of color and of refusing to recognize the complexity of people's relational structures), and would force policy makers, scientists and the public alike to own and contend with their own biases and the implications of repeating history. AIDS activism also learned that it had to coalesce: gay men had to work with lesbians, Latinos with African Americans, people of color with middle-class queers, and wealthy with poor. (Of course, the jury is still out on whether that bridge-building continued once cocktail therapies made AIDS an issue of chronic illness management—for some.) Around civil rights for sexual minorities, that very astute awareness of the historical context was largely lost. As Patton (1995) wrote, gay activists simply sought to extend liberal tradition around civil rights—material and unjust discrimination warranting governmental policy to protect a minority group—without understanding that the political ground had shifted with the rise of the conservative movement, organized with special concern for blunting and rolling back what it viewed as the excesses of the left.

Beyond the importance of historical context, AIDS and civil rights activism taught me the importance of face. Its dynamics and politics possessed symbolic meanings whose process and product were as critical as the more material agenda items over which the identity movements struggled (if not moreso). With HIV and AIDS, the shift of "AIDS victim" to "person living with AIDS" no longer connoted a passive relationship with illness (an inevitable drift to death) that totalized one's being and instead meant AIDS was irreducible to any other aspect of a person's matrix of identities. The way that AIDS was signified made it easier to distance or externalize illness. The face of AIDS appeared as a threat from the distant margins: an emaciated figure inevitably sunken into a bleached out hospital ward bed; or the harrowed expression of a villager in some rustic African village. No less problematic was a face of AIDS that was everywhere all the time, a ubiquitous boogieman without any referent. Like the red menace of the 1920s or the Cold War, threat was everywhere and nowhere. Around civil rights, when the face of sexual minorities signified wealthy white queers or extravagant pride marchers, it was difficult to make oppression register with the general public, but when the images ranged from mutilated victims of bashing to decorated and disabled veterans of military service, the community received greater empathy and had its citizenship and patriotism underscored. When the gays who were seen and embraced in the media became figures the majority could relate to (however problematically), suddenly the face of unease and ugliness was shifted onto vociferous anti-gay activists like Fred Phelps and his Westboro (Kansas) Baptist Church clan.[5]

One final lesson that identity movements have taught me: the need to recognize the false choices of assimilation and separation that so many movements and individuals who are attached/aligned with them must negotiate. For the accommodationist position, dissident movements confront pressure to adopt the social and cultural practices of the majority while generally bracketing their own forms for home or other private venues. Gay people, in this position, are fine so long as they don't threaten or challenge normalized heterosexual institutions like marriage and family, and people of color accommodate themselves by evacuating self-consciousness of their own racial identities and accepting the hegemony of whiteness as the universal/"unmarked" subject position from which to operate. Counterpoised to assimilation, a separatist position maintains autonomy over its ideology, expression and space, excluding the majority but also claiming agency over its own self-exile, as it were. In this view, working-class identity and heritage might be a subject position which someone embraces and builds an epistemology around, and femininity offers a lens (in contrast to patriarchy) where social relations might possess radically different possibilities for collaboration, community, and pathos.

Still, the choice, even the desirability, to assimilate or resist presupposes that movements, or individuals independent from them, operate in contexts (social, cultural, economic, political, institutional, etc.) in which they have agency to pick and choose. What does someone do when the way they perform their identity, consciously, intentionally, or not, makes assimilating moot? What about the contexts where performance of resistant or minority identity can draw violent reaction in a multitude of forms? Activists or people with dissident identities often find themselves torn between "selling out" (accommodating the dominant forces or opposition) and being separatist/radical (rejecting the status quo or establishment). The history of African-American protest rhetoric teaches that such polarity isn't terribly useful or productive. In his 1981 work, "Transcending coercion: The communicative strategies

---

5.   Phelps has gained wide national media attention for leading protests at the funeral for murdered University of Wyoming student Matthew Shepard and most recently at memorials for military personnel who have died in the Iraq war. These protests and deaths, Phelps and his church argue, are the consequence for society's tolerance of sexual diversity.

of black slaves on antebellum plantations," Cal Logue argues for sub-version as a third possibility most immediately evident in such rheto-ric, not a dialectic occupying a middle-ground position between reform and radicalism, but another way that signals a certain rhetorical manip-ulation and cageyness in relation to dominant discourses and practices. In this sense, colonial-era slave narratives or post-Civil War rhetoric that might otherwise appear as oddly genial or lacking in justifiable anger or outrage may be re-read as simultaneously revealing African Americans' strategic study, insight, and coded transfer of knowledge to wider audiences. Such subversive rhetoric also worked to challenge governmental and institutional support of slavery or later highlighted the paradoxes and incongruence of racist practices with national val-ues of equality and citizenship. Queer theory parallels this innovative rhetoric by providing a critical and interpretive method of reading against the grain of texts—bodies, cultural texts, and mass media arti-facts—for imbedded meaning(s) that fly beneath the radar of dominant consumption. A "queering" of the everyday contests any concepts of "normal" or their oppositions as mutually constituting and negotiates safe spaces or contact zones that enable material existence and dampen possibility for discursive or physical violence. From cultural studies, Stuart Hall (1993) offers yet another parallel set of possibilities in his theory on dominant, oppositional, and negotiated modes of interpre-tation. The dominant position accepts the sender's (or more broadly) intended meaning, while the oppositional rejects the preferred mean-ing, opting for a local, individual position. The negotiated position samples from dominant, but adapts it to particular needs and utility. Across these three visions of subversive possibility isn't a position of moderation or reasoned, pragmatic middle-ground; instead, they rec-ognize the power (and the intractability or the sway) of institutions and systems, poach from their rhetorical needs and expectations, and offer a means of change and challenge in contexts where power is tenuous or where the material implications of backlash can be dramatic, horrific, or at minimum daunting.

In writing centers, these very pressures of identity—and their atten-dant politics—are ever-present. A day doesn't go by that somebody doesn't contend with the dilemma of assimilating, going with the flow, or challenging the well-worn path. Often the context involves envision-ing alternatives to hackneyed arguments or unimaginative approaches to writing tasks. But just as frequently, students, tutors, administrators and faculty must confront who they are, whether the identity in question is one from the margins or whether the context forces awareness of one's privilege or position at the center. In those moments, we are forced to contemplate whether to mentor someone to accommodate, to accept often arbitrary "standard" or dominant positions, or to advocate someone to resist, fight back, or challenge them. Again the either/or proposition that movements and activists have faced. Like them, these possibilities are fraught with complications. Almost daily I experience galling moments of homophobia or heterosexism, both overt (epithets hurled at the strangest moments or whispers as my partner and I stroll somewhere among people unaccustomed to folks like us) and more subtle (co-workers gendering me as a gay person, or people assuming I'm straight because my partner has a sex-neutral name). Class bias circulates just as powerfully, from the "tax" first-generation students pay after college (their loans) and the pay differential that that creates for wealthier graduates, to the disproportionate ease middle- and upper-class folks have in accumulating capital (housing, savings for economic security, mobility, etc.) and leveraging it for even greater social, cultural, and economic position. At the same time, my inherent privilege as a white, educated man enables me to benefit from far greater lifetime earnings than most women (and men) and people of color, especially those who remain as working class. Still, the everyday oppression and privilege that circulate in my life is unlike the forms that people of color in the U.S. face. Hearing "faggot" is just as poisonous to an individual or collective psyche as racial or ethnic slurs; of course, these terms have profoundly different histories whose rhetorical impact doesn't just terrorize, but also indexes power and the dynamics of oppression.

Such quotidian experiences might spur someone to battle, but the energy and commitment required to engage such ongoing direct action is just not sustainable, another lesson that any seasoned or weary activist will share. To resist fighting every fight or putting out each fire that pops up prompts those who face oppression to adopt coping strategies that might appear as assimilationist or separatist. But as I've suggested above, those positions are packed with dense dynamics and histories in and of themselves. Kenji Yoshino (2007), in *Covering: The Hidden Assault on Civil Rights*, complicates these positions and offers a framework to explore identity politics, particularly in the context of writing centers. Yoshino revisits Erving Goffman's (1971, 1974) scholarship about face and blends it with memoir, queer theory, and critical legal studies, to share his own journey to make sense of his own conflicted experiences with marginality as a gay, Japanese-American man. He argues gay people, people of color and women often share experiences of self-loathing marked by attempts at conversion, passing, and covering. I would add to Yoshino's analysis any form of oppression for which (mutually constituting) positions of dominance and marginality can be articulated. Conversion involves physical morphing of one identity into another. In Yoshino's case, it involved him literally refusing his nascent homosexuality and instead attempting to live as a straight man. (That conversion obviously didn't take.) The social (and cultural) pressure for people to change class positions is another example of that conversation to which Yoshino speaks. Passing, he explains, involves minimal self-acceptance of one's identity, but making it publicly invisible (or better, illegible for the majority). For Yoshino, passing involved accepting his gay identity, but actively crafting a public persona that prevented anyone from knowing he was different. A biracial or multiethnic person might pass as white and reap the privileges associated with the majority identity. A woman might pass as a man (or vice versa) for a variety of reasons and risks. A queer person might be understood as straight to everyone, and a working-class person might signify another class position. In Yoshino's case, besides bracketing his sexuality, he also refused his ethnic heritage so thoroughly that he was unable, ironically enough, to pass as native in Japan, even though he was just a generation removed. Covering, then, signifies identity in ways that conform to majoritarian expectations: African Americans, in this mindset, may act black, but not too black; women must remain within a range of feminine (though never overtly feminist) codes; and queers may be visible but not threatening. While one might accept "being" a sexual minority, a person of color, or a woman, one may still resist "doing" it, or performing one's identity in ways that challenge the norms of the majority. In Yoshino's case, covering led to the undoing of at least one relationship when he refused to be as queer as his partner demanded (to express affection publicly, to refuse to disclose their relationship, etc.).

The taxonomy that he uses helps complicate the assimilation/separation binary and underscores the case for writing center activism to be read through a lens of subversion. Conversion, passing, and covering are all assimilationist positions that don't challenge the hegemony or rhetorical naturalness of dominant identity formations. To sublimate an identity in favor of another, to render it as illegible to the dominant as well as to those who share the identity, and to mute it in ways that don't challenge the dominant all smack of approaches that are generally conciliatory and internally conflicted, if not out-and-out antipathetic, toward a marginal subject position. One might wonder about someone who attempts to or might surrender, hide, or tone down her or his ethnic or racial, class, gender, sexual, or national identities for the majority position, but the material benefits and privileges offer plausible reasons that shouldn't need to be inventoried. Still, the typical counter-position to assimilation is to advocate an embrace of resistance, or, in the context of writing centers, composition classrooms and writing-intensive courses, to advocate writers embrace their "authentic" voices of home (or to mentor a multiplicity of authentic voices tied to equally diverse discourse communities).

Yoshino's book made me think about how his ideas drew out intersections between identity movements, teaching, composition classrooms and writing centers. Each of these spaces can be quite diverse. Like our wider society, the students being mentored, the tutors and teachers coaching them, and the directors leading those units face the very dynamics that Yoshino writes about. The pressure to convert, pass or cover reveals itself in any number of the identities that these individuals must face in the academy. Celebrated narratives in writing studies—from Rodriguez (1983) to Anzaldúa (2007) and Rose (2005) to hooks (1989)—open up this conversation about the politics of difference and identity for self-awareness, learning and literacies. When I invoke signs like "teacher" or "writer," they possess their own performative and rhetorical demands, but they also intersect with the other subjectivities that make up who I am. The implication of this fluid identity is vertiginous: what role do my other identities play in my identity as a professor, or in what ways do the institutional or rhetorical constraints impact on *how* I perform my identity as a professor? When tutors mentor student writing, they help hone a writer's identity and simultaneously shape themselves as writers *and* consultants. Again, what roles do their other identities factor into the situation? To complicate matters more, mentoring and teaching frequently happen in rhetorical and disciplinary contexts that themselves have conventions and "communities" in their own right that constitute ostensible identities that composition studies has more widely named as "discourse communities." These, then, in turn fold back on, resist, and impact on all the other identities that float around or can be invoked by someone. Like the three-dimensional models of complicated compounds I've seen while wondering lost in some science building, our identities, their relations with one another, and the nebulous whole they create are complicated, integrated, fluid and unstable. That "reality" makes teaching and learning confounding and electric.

MAKING CHANGE: RE-IMAGINING ACTIVISM
IN THE WRITING CENTER

Driving up Twelfth Street, the Center City Philadelphia confluence of bohemia and colonial aura gives way to another world of single room occupancy (SRO) apartment buildings, vacant lots filled with outlaw dumping, and lonely row homes, many left oddly freestanding in the wake of demolished neighbors. In those blocks surrounding Temple University, working-class folks, mainly African American, cleave out existences, not in some abject sensibility, but with a nobility and pride found anywhere. Going south from Center City, one travels through still more working-class white, Latino and African American neighborhoods with considerably less decay, but under just as much economic stress, ever more pronounced as the city's manufacturing, industrial, and military workforces recede into an increasingly distant past. It was within this context that I began to connect the dots of the multifaceted dynamic of social justice in postmodern America. My professors at Iowa and in graduate school had given me theories to understand my own experiences, to put them into a language, and to have greater agency over how they might signify to me or other audiences. In spite of unlearning a good amount of my provincial mindset, I was still narrow. The shame, anger and hurt that I felt, never quite measuring up because of my sexuality and my working-class background, rarely extended outward. My consciousness raising was narcissistic; it was always about me, about my feeling and my sense of connection. Philly taught me about the need for commonwealth, about reckoning with the after effects of segregation and the politics of difference. The individualism that left me compulsively narcissistic, I would learn, also intersected with a wider cultural ethos of individualizing issues, absolving structures, institutions and society from at least minimal complicity or complacency in them. I also learned that undoing the material consequences of division and difference wasn't just a matter of integration, cultural relativity, and equitable distribution (and redistribution) of resources.

Drawn from neighborhoods like Olney, Spring Garden, K&A, or South Philly, Temple students arrived on campus, often the first in their families to attend college, hoping to leverage this experience toward the American meritocratic dream: to do better than their parents before them. In first-year writing or a core humanities course, students would hit a wall. Modes of learning that involved digesting and regurgitating information suddenly weren't useful in contexts where professors required innovative thinking and nuanced argumentation. Students would find themselves having to express themselves under rhetorical and linguistic constraints that their earlier educational experiences hadn't prepared them for and that their professors presumed their knowledge of. Thrust from their comfort zone where they were prepared to tell instructors what they wanted to know, students found themselves in situations with enough room to wallow and held to standards that stifled.

I would see these students again and again in writing centers and classrooms at different institutions where I'd later go on to teach in New York City. The face or identities they brought to campuses butted against the nebulous culture of academic life. Like anyone from the margins, these students could look around and perceive whole ways of being and doing that ran counter to their own. They quickly learned that a premium was placed on those practices. Writing centers became central spaces where I witnessed the struggle to traverse many different worlds. In writing centers, I came to see everyday oppression, natural and exercised without effort: wealthy (white) graduate students from elite undergraduate institutions stunned at the low "quality" of urban students, faculty complaining about illiterate immigrants, instructors responding in offensive and abusive ways on papers, students parroting hate speech as effortless stock rhetoric, and tutors complaining about the hygiene of clients. Writing centers also witness magical, rich moments: consultants mentoring faculty about responding to student writing in productive ways; students sharing life stories that leave tutors in tears, laughter, anger; students bounding in with news of improved grades; tutors learning as much about a student's home language and culture as his mentoring shares about academic forms of argumentation.

Whether a situation presents "non-traditional" students coming to terms with academic demands or a dynamic offers a glimpse at more abstract forces at play, the writing center is a place to make a more immediate, different impact than conventional activism. The writing center and the actors in play within it put into practice what Antonio Gramsci (1971) would call organic intellectualism–a form of mentoring that's rooted in a learner's everyday needs. To commingle a pedagogy of empowerment with community building and consciousness raising was a praxis not entirely different from conventional activism. I remember Annisa, a graduate student and aspiring New York City high school teacher who was confounded by the essay component of the state's certification test. By reassuring her and demystifying the prompt and learning goals (not teaching her a template, but mentoring her to plan and organize her thoughts), we worked together to displace her anxiety and tapped into her sardonic, but playful way of thinking. We imagined her having a conversation with her readers, leading them toward her criticisms by poking fun and teasing. As her voice and affect began to shine through, her confidence grew, and she eventually re-took her exams, passing with a wide margin. I also remember Camille, another graduate student and one of my first consultants. Doubt and weak self-confidence dogged her. In her I noticed a "natural" affinity to establish rapport and dig in with a student; students connected with her because she was "real" and lacked pretense. From her tutoring and classroom instruction experiences along with a good deal of prodding from my colleagues, she took a chance to go on for more advanced graduate study. She met every challenge, but invariably approached each with a wistful insecurity that I recognized in myself as well. I don't mention these instances to trumpet my own glory; instead, they signal the difference a person can make, change that's lasting, change that's slow, change that doesn't necessarily announce itself. Moreover, in the writing centers where I've worked, community happens in ways that can't be anticipated, not so much in the cliquey adolescent sort of manner, but more in the spirit of tutors coming together for mutual support of one another and students alike.

Of course, students of all stripes use writing centers, and they persist in a variety of contexts with wide-ranging institutional support and positioning. All students find themselves learning the cultural capital to be effective participants in academic life, but the distances that some must traverse can be quite different. In an academy where the discursive practices of the middle class dominate, the "standards" aren't so alien when the language and ways of knowing and doing are so proximate to people's existing cultural capital. For students whose cultural capital doesn't neighbor the mainstream, they encounter a learning situation fraught with complexity: Do they surrender their code for another alien one? Do they resist and face the material and symbolic consequences of not fitting in? Do they negotiate some sort of middle ground? How might they subvert all these confining possibilities? In answering these questions, the phenomenon of face or identity literally comes to the front in the writing center. Like identity movements, people in education and those in writing centers specifically must negotiate a common ground of self and Other, of audience and rhetorical purpose. It is both a product and process that is inextricably political.

That very negotiation is the heart of this book. Following on Yoshino's and my own earlier work, it will present theories of specific aspects of identity dominant in writing centers in the U.S., map the dynamics that produce faces that range from assimilationist to separatist, and posit possibilities for subverting or queering them. *Facing the Center* focuses on identities and politics most central in our national context, faces whose politics have the greatest material consequences, even though they are not exhaustive to the possibilities.[6] Chapter 2 takes up the charge Victor Villanueva (2003, 2006) has made (and Frankie Condon (2007) has extended to writing centers) to place the dynamics of race at the center of discussion and analysis. Working from a scenario where a client challenges a tutor's authority on the basis of her race, the chapter points out people of color cannot convert their racial identities to the majority–they cannot *become* the white majority (and I doubt most would choose to become white if they could). People with privileged racial identities, far from operating from positions of unmarked bodies, signify themselves in ways that require naming and owning. Negotiating racial identity and structural racism forces the question of passing, covering, or subverting. An assimilationist approach forces Others to reify dominant society's skepticism and to perpetuate the presumption of white ethos. To be anti-assimilationist, on the flipside, is to force a never-ending campaign of teaching, at best, or contesting people's prejudices, both of which take time away from other lines of collaboration. While activists and Others in writing centers cannot wish away this work, they must also affirm the need to account for how

---

6.   As someone with a differently-abled sister, I personally understand this gap in the book's coverage. Just as no one element of identity can be foundational or a linchpin to "true" epistemology, no amount of cataloging would capture every face that a writing center encounters. Instead, I stand by my initial call to place identity at the center, inviting indexing of its manifestations however, wherever possible.

race signifies people before they have a chance to signify themselves, and that process proceeds with the cumulative history of race relations in the United States. Subversion would involve confronting structural racism by creating spaces and occasions to self-reflect and question assumptions about race and its consequences for interaction.

Chapter 3 explores the face of class in the writing center. I question: How does class become legible in a writing center? Are there class-coded ways of presenting face, or of trying to compensate for it? What makes somebody signify her or his class position? In cultural and composition studies, there is a long history of accounting for the ways in which one's class position impacts literacy as well as teaching and learning (For more, see Rose 2005, Harris 1997, Shor 1992, Rodriguez 1983, hooks 1989 and 1994, Shaughnessy 1997, Williams 1983, and Willis 1981), but writing center scholarship has remained largely silent on the subject and its dynamics for tutoring. The contemporary emergence of most writing centers dovetails with the influx of first-generation college students, who often arrive on campuses with differential academic capital. This mismatch often positions writing centers as remedial sites that "fix" problematic students, and they in turn quickly learn how institutions view them as deficient. In addition, students come to view the codes with which they speak and write as part of a larger set of hurdles to overcome in order to lift themselves into the middle class and its economic security. Their working-class identities are viewed as suspect or as a handicap to the meritocractic dream of generational improvement. Students (and working-class faculty and staff, for that matter) often experience a process of coming to be ashamed of their upbringing or community roots (LeCourt 2006). Working-class people also learn that education isn't supposed to broaden one's mind or make them better citizens (uses of education that are natural to upper classes); rather, education takes on an overriding vocational or utilitarian thrust, uses that further encode class status. Complicating matters, it is often not entirely clear just how conscious working-class students, tutors and professionals are of their roots since most people in the U.S. identify as middle class, even if that claim is tenable or arguable. Unlike race and ethnicity, our society places a premium on class conversion, and lacking that, many face lifelong processes of passing, covering, and even using subversion. Rarely do we see occasions where one's working-class identity is celebrated as either a code or set of experiences valued widely in the academy or writing center. Instead, it is usually viewed as a burden to overcome.

Following this discussion of class, I revisit my earlier work on sexuality in the writing center in Chapter 4. Writing centers are often positioned as feminist spaces because their pedagogy is conventionally collaborative, non-competitive, and egalitarian (Lutes 2002; Woolbright 2003; Welch 1999). They are also spaces where gender and sexual politics are present throughout conference interaction and diffused throughout wider dynamics. From the ways in which sexual identities are normalized to the gendered assumptions that are invoked, performances are never natural or neutral, and they make the pragmatics of conferences and everyday life in writing centers rich and complex. Here, conforming to, rejecting or subverting conventions of gender or sexuality are cliché to academic culture and anathema in certain circumstances.

The needs and issues attendant to non-native English writers are frequent objects of discussion in writing centers, particularly where international and immigrant students have increasing campus presence. In Chapter 5, I focus on the face nationality creates for writing centers. For international and immigrant students, there is an intense desire to pass as "real" Americans – not to appear as an outsider in the midst of conventional students. For many international students, the desire to blend in can be aided by economic privilege, whereas for many immigrant students, the tug of home community complicates the desire to assimilate. Each group must contend with face, but the stakes are differential. Frequently, interaction is predicated on banking American English codes and practices, implying that they are static and non-responsive to negotiated use (that Americans are incapable of hearing accent or dialect). Similar to its historical positioning, writing centers have reacted to the presence of the ESL writers as "problems" to "fix."

The book closes by returning to the writing center and exploring the face and identity politics the units and the professionals within them must negotiate. For this chapter, I revisit how writing centers themselves assume a sort of sub-institutional identity that has its own politics. Just as actors who come into writing centers must negotiate the politics of face, the sites themselves contend with a complex dynamic that reflects their own unique historical positions. Some centers are positioned within academic units, as marginalized appendages to composition or literature departments or as vaunted centers for teaching and learning. Still other centers are located within wider student support service units, subject to academic corporatist pressures and whims. Depending on their positioning, centers assume accommodationist relationships to their "parent" units, or they can be sites of resistance to or subversion of the larger institution. These centers become advocates (or activists) for change in academic culture, often local and organic. Viewed from a different angle, writing centers can be peer-centered, staffed with advanced undergraduates, or they can be virtual apprenticeship shops, locations where graduate students learn valuable teaching lessons to apply as conventional classroom teachers. Directorship and staffing differs across institutions: professional guidance can range from research and teaching faculty, to full-time administrators and graduate students. Credentials and performance expectations can vary from advanced degrees and minimal participation to terminal degrees and regimented time "booked" in the spaces. The "who" of writing centers, then, can speak volumes about how they are positioned and valued, but the calculus is by no means simple.

NOTES TOWARD A CRITICAL CITIZENSHIP

This book places a premium on viewing writing centers as sites for activism and social change. Positioned that way, I know the sentiment can have a certain messianic zeal. I've become a firm believer in micro-shifts culminating in slow revolutions. Earthquakes don't happen as the result of sudden ruptures; rather, the slippages of tectonic plates occur as the product of slow, virtually invisible, constantly building pressure. Social change just will not happen with the snap of fingers or the loudest of protest screams. To channel Malcolm Gladwell (2002) for a moment, tipping points happen at unexpected moments and can't be predicted, *per se*, but they build from *something*, from some spur. These kicks and nudges have to be understood in relation to and acting on wider, more abstract forces of the society, economics, and culture, each of them further poaching and reacting to one another. It's an amorphous whole that's hard to conceptualize and even more difficult to find a tangible outlet for. Where is racism located and owned? What's the home for class privilege or gender bias? From whom do I seek redress for heterosexism or ethnocentric teaching? Oppression is ubiquitous yet ethereal. To combat oppression is just as local and individual as it is global and collective.

In *The Twilight of Equality?: Neoliberalism, Cultural Politics, and the Attack on Democracy*, Lisa Duggan (2004) analyzes the contemporary impasse of progressive activism and argues the roots to its failures are dynamic. Part of the fault rests with what she argues is a widespread acquiescence to neoliberal hegemony. This metanarrative goes beyond mere ideology and offers a totalizing worldview that's taken by society as the natural order of things, the way the world ought to be is never questioned or doubted. Under neoliberalism, corporate and government policies create the best possible conditions for global capitalism as well as for the concentration of wealth and resources. Transnational corporations are viewed as benevolent entities, and awareness of and outrage toward their tendencies to flout human rights, labor organizing, living wages, or progressive environmental policy are suppressed or minimized, all the easier when media outlets are subsidiaries of larger, nebulous organizations. Companies like ExxonMobil, General Electric and Nike transcend state and national boundaries and are driven to maximize profit for shareholders by any means possible. Consumers become complicit in neoliberalism by demanding cheap prices, broad choices, wide opportunity for consumption even as their real-time wages remain stagnant and dissipate and as they refuse to (or are unable to) question the conditions that give rise to them. To challenge neoliberalism is tantamount to waging "class warfare" or advocating economic nationalism by privileging the economic over other forms of division or identity.

Identity movements are themselves by-products of these post-industrial economic and social shifts. As middle-class ideals of domesticity yielded to pressures for a wider range of living and earning options for women and men alike, gender norms were re-imagined, and as racial and ethnic minorities butted against civic promises and uncivil reality, contradictions needed to be reconciled. Identity movements "protest. . . exclusions from national citizenship or civic participation, and against the hierarchies of family life" (Duggan 2004, 7). In their movement for social inclusion, Duggan adds, identity movements "fight for equality without any referent to the material conditions that impact upon it" (XVIII). Hence, the paradox Duggan maps: the very components of identity on which this book focuses—race, class, sex, and nationality—wouldn't have become the objects of identity movements without shifts in economic relations, yet the very complexity of identity under which neoliberalism masks itself in no small measure—the fragmentary subject of postmodernity—wouldn't be possible without individuals coalescing into movements that seek greater social and cultural inclusion, imagine and view society in distinct terms, and present possibilities that ironically challenge hegemony. Curiously, challenging neoliberalism, Duggan argues, depends on fostering a pedagogy rooted in critical citizenship, one that embraces multiculturalism and the different terministic lenses it offers, but one that fosters a discriminating mindset toward macroeconomic forces. A progressive "revolution" has been staved off by a population unable to sustain criticism of the economy and identity movements not capable of coalescing as united front.

As the cliché goes, the revolution won't be televised, and it likely isn't going to ignite in the writing center or some other calculated site. Progressive teaching or mentoring doesn't embrace multiculturalism for the sake of doing so or raise consciousness just to expand possibilities. By helping anyone become aware of difference, the hegemonic status of the same, the standard, is challenged. It revives a notion of citizenship where active engagement supplants passive consent. That pedagogical context involves thinking, writing, talking; it begs for debating where agreement and conflict arise in productive, rich, and uncomfortable ways. Not every session will be an occasion to unpack identity politics, and not every staff meeting, tutor training or consulting course will focus on social justice and possibilities of action in writing centers. But identity and the politics of negotiation and face are always present and require inventory and mapping. I offer this text as a starting point, launching pad, or intervention in conversations yet to begin, in those that are ongoing, or in ones that have passed.

INTERCHAPTER 1

A READER'S GUIDE TO THE INTERCHAPTERS:

Over the years, I've been inspired by texts in composition and writing center studies that attempt to transcend the boundaries of conventional chapters or essays in collections. My most direct influences have been Donna LeCourt's (2004) self-reflections on her experiences growing up working class in Boston and her conscious work to encode her language and wider performance as signifying something other than the economic roots from which she came. Joe Harris (1997) writes in a similar vein in his review of composition studies scholarship since the late 1960s. He channels his own working-class experiences as fodder to push and extend his argument. Mark Hurlbert and Michael Blitz (1991) follow a different tack in their edited collection, turning to transcripts to provide opportunities for texts to apply theoretical lessons learned.

As I've considered this text, I've been deeply conflicted about the dominance and privilege that my voice and narrative takes on, particularly in the context of a monograph that's as much about disrupting the face at the center as it about facing the center, in writing centers, composition studies, and beyond. In that sense of center as uninterrogated, privileged, and unmarked, I'm an author who ironically calls for attention to the fluidity and liminality of the center, margin, and face, even as I have the authority and agency to easily embody and perform each of those positions. I am—I do—the very postmodern identities that I call for the field to inventory and problem-pose. But, while I am queer and celebrate my working-class roots, my material and ideological reality today is thoroughly privileged. My authority and expertise are granted, for the most part, by audiences who read my body and affect as socio-cultural markers for ethos. Though I make attempts to qualify and signal the lens through which I perceive the world (and it me), I fear suggesting my experiences are foundational or somehow transcendent. To check or bracket them and to complicate my narrative, I sought an admittedly convenient sample of writing consultants who have worked with me or who have spoken to me at conferences over the years and who might push what I'm arguing or invite further dialogue with readers.

Like the scenarios that lead off each chapter, I imagine this text being fodder for tutor education courses or wider conversations among new and experienced classroom teachers. Our professional convention workshops and listserv conversations frequently get requests and postings asking for pragmatic advice. Too often these dialogues are more about exchanging recipes and how-to's as opposed to fostering deeper thinking and problem-posing. Anne Ellen Geller (2005) understands this tension as one of timing, where the pressure to beat the clock or meet the demands of the moment (fungible time) too often eclipses or denies occasions to dig deep and revel in the potential of the moment. These interchapters will work to model a different way of doing critical exchange. Often, it will not even be about a right or wrong answer, but thinking differently through a new set of eyes. My own responses to what these consultants have to say should not be read as the final word; rather, my hope is to offer them as a model and launching pad for putting into practice the very ideas and themes that each chapter seeks to present.

* * *

Michelle Solomon: New York City English teacher; former writing center tutor at SUNY Stony Brook and Long Island University/Brooklyn

You discuss "white, middle-class, straight, American privileged colleagues" who might wonder "why 'they' (the Others) weren't more present." At what point would my own actions be seen as "embracing" or "reflecting" the Other? I expect the same level of hard work and professionalism not only in the students I tutor, but in the students I teach in the classroom. I expect work to be done well and on time, regardless of background (with the understanding that I am always available to those who need it because of background). I choose texts that reflect "the Other," and populations who struggle and whose voices are not always heard by dominant populations. I assign writing assignments that allow students to write about their background, their families, their struggles, themselves. I give a voice to as many of my students as I can, inexperienced teacher as I am. Yet I know that more is expected of me, simply because I am not an Other. I expect the students whom I tutor to come to the writing center prepared to work. I'm still trying to determine how much of their Othered background I should pay attention to, if I should pay attention to it at all. The truth of the matter is that their Other status is immaterial to me from the standpoint that I still expect my students to work, and only really consider that background if it affects their work in some capacity.

I hear both tension and frustration in Michelle's words. Those feelings are real and legitimate and experienced by almost every consultant and teacher at one time or another. I suspect the frustration comes in the gulf between her expectations and investment and those that her students possess. In writing centers and composition courses, tutors and instructors work to negotiate where our students are rather than where we'd like to be. In that sense, we begin to channel the improvisational spirit that Beth Boquet (1999) writes about so cogently, but I've also become more comfortable negotiating demands and expectations with students on the premise that I've got an obligation to tap into their own developmental motives and needs as well as to think about how I can make what they need to write about relevant to their personal and collective interests. If we view the context of writing, learning, and teaching through our students' eyes, instead of battling them on our terms, then how can we create a common, even middle, ground?

Michelle also seems frustrated by the dynamics of the Other. I hear a hint of a desire to find a teaching and learning space that's beyond the politics of Other (and same/privilege), that's exterior to "work" or whatever wider learning we facilitate in our classrooms and conferences. I just don't buy that we can get beyond identity however it's expressed in our classrooms or consulting sessions. What would that world look and feel like? How would we go about suspending who we are to engage any learning? Of course, we never interact with our environments fully cognizant of how our identities make knowing possible, but we're always already who we are. It'd be, I suppose, a compelling learning environment to suspend awareness that I'm gay, a man, a professor—to flick a switch and turn any one or set of them off—but I don't see any utility in such exercises. Instead, I think what's more powerful in what Michelle is struggling with is how we address the experience gulfs between ourselves and others. I'm drawn to the lessons that Nancy Grimm teaches in her 1999 work, *Good Intentions: Writing Center Work for Postmodern Times*, in which she teaches us to think about how we change our teaching and learning relationships from uncomplicated linear transactions between institutions and individuals and toward interaction that's rooted in being cultural informants. What would her classroom or tutoring sessions look like if they were mutually informing, enabling her students to shape and communicate knowledge through their experiences for her as a teachable audience and vice versus? What might those conversations look like if she worked toward collaborative learning within subsets and across plenary groups of students?

2

FACING RACE AND ETHNICITY
IN THE WRITING CENTER

Scene 1: An African American graduate student sits down with her student, an immigrant Russian undergraduate working on a paper for an upper-level writing requirement. The student has inflected a current events paper with what the tutor perceives as racist rhetoric. When she pushes the student to think about her argumentation, the student says she thought her tutor was going to be one of the white tutors and questions her tutor's qualifications. On later reflection the tutor says that her maturity and experience (she's a returning student who has spent a number of years as a corporate trainer) kept her from reacting to the student and chalked it up to a combination of immaturity and a lack of cultural knowledge. The tutor diffuses the situation by speaking to her qualifications and life history.

Scene 2: A writing center prides itself for having a great deal of racial, gender, cultural, economic, and academic diversity. The director jokes, "We're like a Benetton ad for writing centers." But on deeper reflection he begins to realize that "problem tutors" are ones who don't conform to the ideal face that the space has. What does it mean to have diversity commingle with a homogenized sense of performativity? What's the place for a tutor whose affect doesn't fit into an institutional culture dominated by "model minorities"?

Over the years, when I've shared this first scenario with writing center audiences, the typical reaction has been disbelief. Surely, people say, this tutor misunderstood the student. Surely, they respond, everything isn't as it seems, or as bad as it appears; more details would get to the heart of the problem, beyond the hasty conclusion that race was at issue. Racism couldn't be the problem, they protest. Instead, the issue, they earnestly intone, has to be related to interpersonal tension, cultural misunderstanding, hypersensitive individuals. Curiously, the doubters, over and over again, were white like me, yet in their initial reaction to explain away race, I always wondered whether they recognized their power—our agency, authority, gumption—in such rhetorical moves. I wondered about their impact on people of color in our immediate company or those who are colleagues, staff and clients back on campus, those who hear and experience their identities as vantage points inevitably suspect while their white interlocutors' perspectives are beyond reproach. Our impulse around race was to doubt rather than believe what my former tutor had told me. We lacked the very capacity or imagination to view an experience through a different set of eyes, the ones my tutor experienced in very real ways. I wondered what it said more deeply about teachers' and tutors' ability to suspend judgment while responding to student writing: How many of us chided and corrected ("Sorry, you're getting this wrong!" before we affirmed and applauded ("I hear you saying this" or "I like that. Could you say more?")? Of course, it's easy for me to sit back, all sanctimonious, and act like I haven't played the very same game myself, to deny and doubt or to arbitrate a person of color's experience of everyday racism. But I have, more often than I'd like to admit. I'm just as guilty as the next person, wielding whatever privilege comes easily and naturally to me with little thought to its immediate and long-term consequences.

As a white person, I know the knee-jerk compulsion to pretend, to refuse race, even racism, are at play. "Surely," I've said, "You must be getting this wrong." "Don't you think you're being just a bit too sensitive?" I've challenged. Not too long ago, a graduate student called me out on my own discomfort dealing with race, having noticed my nonverbal "tells." He had observed me get flushed talking about racial tension when the conversations weren't on my own terms, under my control. My pale pink face would grow red at flash points of conflict and discomfort. This graduate student forced me to reflect on my own everyday practices. I realized that I'm not uncomfortable taking on conflict when it's couched in low-stakes discussions. I tend toward warm and fuzzy conversations about diversity that raise consciousness but rarely upset or threaten—especially myself. I plant seeds and raise questions, the answers and resolutions to which aren't really meant to be hashed out face to face or which really aren't offered for deep thinking in the moment. Such talk fails to create space for people to get real with one another and instead skims the surface, satisfying no one. But the alternatives, flashpoints for challenge and conflict, feel too chaotic and risky and leave me not knowing how to facilitate substantive dialogue without traumatizing those involved. How do we get real without creating too much discomfort? Moreover, how do we tap those feelings as fodder for sustainable learning and teaching? Those moments of grinding tension or frustration often produce powerful breakthroughs from which change and growth can flourish.

My own journey to understand the identity politics of race didn't just begin with a student calling me out on my own insecurities and the ways I put them into practice. Rather, coming to an awareness of my whiteness and the privilege it confers as natural, through institutions and my own individual actions, has taught me that my own ways of knowing and doing race must be starting points for any activism I advocate. Growing up in Iowa couldn't have provided an environment more racially homogeneous, yet throughout my childhood in a working-class family, racism was a constant companion. My family's own paycheck-to-paycheck existence and periods on public assistance—registers of our material and economic instability—were always counterbalanced by discourses that we, at least, had it better (were better) than "them," people of color. My grandfather's alcoholism never signified as an individual failing, but as a register of his slide from white propriety into depravity with black folks whose bars he'd get drunk in and stumble home from. For her part, my grandmother never spoke with any awareness of her lifetime spent as one of the first female meat-cutters at Oscar Mayer; instead, night after night, year after year, she'd take pride in performing as a matriarchal Archie Bunker, loudly and vulgarly complaining about the African Americans who shared a production line with her. My family never talked about or processed the disjunction between her words and her actions, like when she'd cook or care for an African American co-worker hurt on the job or another who had lost a partner. As my dad gained access to a union job and began working his way up through the local leadership, our family drifted from its clannish, multigenerational, extended network and toward a lower-middle-class, blue collar existence (with our own home, and nuclear family routines separate from the rest of our relatives). I saw dad go off and work and socialize with African American co-workers and fellow union members; slowly, the racist discourse diminished and disappeared as the family changed and our lives extended into different worlds, with support systems that introduced us to other experiences. Proximity to others had an impact, though I don't know that the pedagogy of it all was ever fully conscious. In the early to mid-1980s, the farm crisis and recession decimated the Quad Cities' manufacturing sector, intensifying the existing poverty and broadening the suffering. No longer could economic struggles be forgotten as *just* a problem endemic to African Americans; with the deepening social problems, people began to question those historical explanations. As times improved and populations moved on, however, the promise of deeper and broad-based questioning dissipated for another day.

The first chapter alludes to my early experiences with activism and how they provided searing lessons about racial identity politics. I never knew a time when HIV and AIDS weren't always about race and racism and their thoroughly systemic dynamics. If the face of AIDS through its first decade wasn't routinely offered up and dismissed as gay, that personification was constructed as African or Caribbean. White America was assured that HIV was a consequence, inevitable at that, of identities and geographies (often conflated with one another). Middle-class, white America had nothing to worry about because its sexual propriety secured its immunity; only "the gays" and "the blacks," pathological, hypersexual, and disease-prone as they were symbolically constructed in mainstream discourses, were the ones at risk, who needed to be contained and regulated. In Reagan/Bush America, a global health pandemic became an ongoing morality play whose lessons were elastic and pliable to any population or figure that popped up to challenge or dislodge the face of AIDS. Injecting drug users, just as often white as of color, were cast as flawed and inherently health-compromised creatures, exiles from the middle class. Even ostensibly heterosexual (and white) seropositive people came to signify as never quite so, even "pseudo-homo," because they dared to have unprotected sex outside the sanctity of the nuclear family and its sexual politics. As the epidemic drifted into its third decade and health care developed protocols that extended life, white activists drifted away from direct interest, assuming the experiences of those with middle-class access to treatment was shared by poorer people (disproportionately people of color).

Beyond the work of HIV and AIDS education and activism, I learned that even civil rights activism was charged with racialized politics, ironically enough. For white gay activists, combating sexuality-based discrimination precluded any consideration of the racial history of civil rights in the U.S. My colleagues were shocked and amazed to discover a mainstream society ready, willing, and able to discriminate, to marginalize, and to demonize when confronted with the possibility that another axis of its privilege was coming under scrutiny. Veteran civil rights activists would ask, rhetorically, over and over again, "Where were you folks when…?" They knew, too well, that white society was always quite ready to proclaim the country "post-race" and roll back, by popular vote, laws and judicial decisions designed to protect the minority from the majority and to mitigate the consequences of long (and continuing) practices of discrimination. But because queer activists couldn't see the connections between forms of oppression, they couldn't connect the genealogy of racism and xenophobia against people of color with what the LGBT community was facing. What's more, they couldn't see anti-gay legislation as a back door, a chink in the wall of liberal-era efforts to diminish and mitigate a cumulative history of discrimination. Queers didn't connect the dots between Colorado's Amendment 2 and the Defense of Marriage Act and ongoing attempts to roll back affirmative action, voting rights, desegregation policy, and wider social integration. Those were, my fellow activists would assure me, completely separate and unrelated. No small wonder that African and Latino Americans saw the gay community as wholly white, even when they knew people of color as part of our collective, and it wasn't surprising that queers of color identified more intensely with populations defined by race. Coming out of those experiences in the early 1990s, my own whiteness was never more fully legible to me, in all its offensive and natural privilege, than when I worked as an activist and tried to make change happen.

When I landed in writing centers after that other life and its disillusionment and began another journey in the academy, I saw the same racial tensions and possibilities and once again naïvely thought fundamental change was possible. Writing centers, I thought, could be sites for activism; organic, sustainable, even broader change could be had there, though it had eluded me elsewhere. Years later, I'm still hopeful, but I now know that such labor results in shifts that are tremendously local, plodding, and at times, fleeting. The first scenario I presented at the beginning of this chapter is rich with possibilities for promoting anti-racism work in writing centers. Allia, the tutor who experienced the conflict, was compelled to prove her ethos in ways that white people just are never compelled to do in the same way. That performance reflected her sophistication and experience, a lifetime of doing that dance over and over and over again. Allia could respond because she had a register of responses, representing a rhetorical readiness that was socially constructed and exclusive to African Americans, and invoked where and when symbolic and material success weren't assured. As

Allia once she told me, confronting every offense that comes down the pike is exhausting; she could have, justifiably, gotten angry, growled an equally off-putting response, or directly confronted the moment of racism. Instead, she chose to work around it. Allia responded to the student in neither a genial nor a confrontational manner, but another, subversive way, one which refused the marginalizing positioning implicit in the student's discourse and one which enacted the very professionalism and dignity the student had attempted to strip. Just as striking as what Allia reported as her response was the implication of just how much of our society's racism this immigrant had internalized in her relatively short time in the country, and how it commingled with the politics of race and difference in her homeland. This student was performing everyday American attitudes and practices toward race in an overt way that "natives" enact in more subtle, though no less offensive ways. What if the student were a person of color confronting identity politics from a tutor possessing racial privilege? In what ways does everyday practice delegitimize the student's experiences from a racial standpoint? How often has a student been told that experiences with race were off base, that they must be misunderstanding or misconstruing a situation? In what ways do we police real experiences with race and racism (or any form of oppression) in our writing centers?

Beyond the everyday struggle for people of color—whether they're tutors or clients in writing centers or classrooms across the curriculum—to learn, assert, or contest ethos, from the words they produce to the essays and other writing they create, there's an ongoing struggle over face they must confront. Which faces are permitted and tolerated and which ones face scrutiny, challenge or oppression? The opening scene gets at dynamics that operate in understated ways in writing centers and across college campuses. "Changing the face of" is a recurrent refrain from diversity panels at professional conferences or in articles that take up the ongoing under-representation of people of color in writing centers, composition, and the academy at large. I take pride in the staff of my writing centers mirroring our student bodies, but this reality is more a consequence of my institutional context than strategic work on my part. At more homogeneous colleges and universities, the effort must be more sustained to get similar results. But regardless of whether we have a diverse writing center or not—whether we have a critical mass of people of color that, by virtue of presence, challenge the hegemony of race as ordinarily practiced—we still must create a space to dig into how racial identity politics play out in writing centers and beyond, and how they affect the myriad issues around learning to write. We must, I contend, uncover the hidden curriculum of race in education, the one that inscribes a racialized margin and center. We must think about how our practices represent a pedagogy of conduct that dominates and enacts privilege by teaching codes that naturalize the very people who benefit from it, perform it, signify it. People who teach in writing centers or composition courses must question how we interrogate ways of signifying, how these processes make possible both center and margin, and how that dichotomy can be re-imagined as a range of possible identities to which people can have strategic rhetorical positions.

As much as this book begs consideration of the face of writing centers—what they are—such reflection doesn't get to the heart of what I'm advocating. The Benetton ad writing center might exist as an ideal and a reality, but it might still be rife with unresolved identity politics around race. In other words, being multiracial (or inclusive in any number of other ways) doesn't get into how race (or any other identity intrinsic to who we are) gets played out or acted on in everyday practice. A multiracial writing center might foster a learning environment that naturalizes a monocultural approach to rhetoric and expression, while a writing center less racially diverse might actively create spaces for conversation where learners and tutors alike challenge, explore, or scaffold to and from multiple linguistic, argumentation, and genre traditions. Although writing centers and composition classrooms can often get students and teachers past an obsessive attention to products and redirect our focus toward process, the very same negotiation needs to happen around our racial identity politics. Having diversity isn't enough or a necessary end; instead, we need to process whether and how it happens and to what consequence. As a means of providing a common language and framework by which to understand race, I'll first bridge theory on race to critical race conversations in writing center and composition studies. With that shared background, I argue that people of color often face pressure to accommodate to naturalized white codes of rhetorical expression, to perform them as stable, ahistorical standards. Juxtaposed to that hegemonic curriculum, my discussion then advocates oppositional or subversion codes, not as equivalent means of expression without consequences, but as codes that enable students and consultants to view communication as involving strategic choices over which they ought to have agency.

THEORIZING RACE AND THE WRITING CENTER

Linda Alcoff argues race and gender are forms of identity that are visible on our bodies, making them fundamental to how we experience the world: "Visibility is both the means of segregating and oppressing human groups and the means of manifesting unity and resistance" (2006, 7).[7] While I challenge Alcoff's belief that other forms of identity don't have the same visibility and foundationalism as race and gender, I will concede that their histories and material experiences are profoundly different. Before we can understand how assimilation, opposition, and resistance impact the face of race in writing centers and other learning contexts, it's critical to explore what's meant by race and to turn that insight to composition and writing center studies.

Sociologists Michael Omi and Howard Winant (1986) map the history of racial theory and argue for a framework that they name "racial formation." They point out that modern responses to race have ranged from the biological and ethnic to class and national understandings.[8] In each theory, race is made ancillary to other forms of identity; that is, those explanations offer other traits as foundational to society. Omi and Winant argue that race, like any other form of identity, needs to be viewed as a primary means by which society is organized. Put another way, our discourses and practices can't be understood without the role of race factored into any analysis; that any understanding without it is partial and incomplete, that race is irreducible to other historical features of identity and domination as well as they to it.[9]

Omi and Winant (1986) posit the ethnicity model as the dominant paradigm by which race is understood in the U.S. It understands race as one social category among many possible across ethnic groups. The ethnicity model places emphasis on the notion of collectivity and has its roots in the study of voluntary or forced (slavery) immigration in European and American contexts. The paradigm held that assimilation led to a dynamic merging of ethnic identities with new American ones. However, research challenged the validity of this model as evidence

7.   I thank an anonymous reviewer for pointing me to Alcoff and reminding me of her importance to discussions of identity politics.
8.   Omi and Winant don't dwell on the biological paradigm very long because it predated social scientific work on race. Moreover, the belief system conflated genuine physiological differences with racist notions of social and cultural superiority and inferiority.
9.   This framing intentionally echoes Eve Sedgwick's (1990) literary criticism vis-à-vis sexuality.

mounted that assimilation often didn't happen or happened in less than complete ways. By the 1950s, waves of earlier immigrants seemed to have been incorporated by wider society, while African Americans, whose arrival predated most immigrants, still struggled to eke out any minimal sense of integration. At the same time, those very immigrants, though identifying as American, still maintained rich community and cultural identities rooted in ethnic origins. In stark contrast, the very same community ties and cultural practices among people of color were viewed with suspicion and, frequently enough, attempts at suppression or, from time to time, imitation and appropriation. If the ethnic model's assumption of assimilation was correct, black people should have long since been integrated smoothly; the reality was, of course, at the height of Jim Crow segregation, dramatically different. Countering this assimilationist-ethnicity paradigm—that race and ethnicity might someday give way to an amorphous national identity—a cultural pluralist-ethnicity position emerged in relation to the mid-century civil rights movement. It accepted the persistence of multiple racial and ethnic identities and sought public policy to mollify the effects of difference and to, in effect, bracket the historical precedents to discrimination and anti-pluralism.

Beyond these mainstream views of race, more critical theories also have emerged, though they haven't challenged the dominance of the ethnic model, particularly in the domain of governmental policy, and more narrowly in relation to education and pedagogy. One model argues that race is a product of class struggle, that it's an invention to divide workers from one another, building in inherent and structural benefits and losses for whites and blacks alike. In some sectors, white earning power is elevated by exclusion of and discrimination against people of color, ostensibly reducing the labor pool arbitrarily and enabling a concentration and greater earning power for white workers. Beyond this Marxist understanding of race, Omi and Winant (1986) also detail a model that focuses on the nexus of nationality and colonialism, where race is the product of nations working to dominate or oppress one another. Domestically, "internal colonialism" works on the premise that groups of people are segregated from one another, forms of domination and resistance emerge, and institutional structures develop in reaction to them. Urban ghettos came into existence as the most legible instances of colonialism, ranging from attempts to confine African Americans within them through redlining and other

predatory housing practices, to well-meaning liberal outreach programs to save people from poverty by means of banking curricula
meant to invest populations with "necessary" skills and educational
capital for self-improvement.

Omi and Winant (1986) fault these class- and colonialism-focused
theories of race for misunderstanding race as a concept rooted in some
nebulous empirical reality, rather than as a term rooted in a pliable
meaning tied to particular histories. These authors believe that, for
all the interrogation of how race operates, its root causes or origins,
it has always been understood as a category that "broader" ones sub-
sume, rendering the complexity and fundamentals of race unexamined
(13). Instead, they advocate understanding race in a different way, as a
"formed" entity.

> Race is indeed a pre-eminently *sociohistorical* concept. Racial categories and
> the meaning of race are given concrete expression by the specific social rela-
> tions and historical context in which they are embedded. Racial meanings
> have varied tremendously over time and between different societies. (Omi
> and Winant 1986, 60)

Race, in Omi and Winant's terms, is inherently a social construction,
one not ever settled, but one constantly in a fluid state. They view race
as a contested term, a formation that:

> Refer[s] to the process by which social, economic and political forces deter-
> mine the content and importance of racial categories, and by which they are
> in turn shaped by racial meanings. Crucial to this formation is the treatment
> of race as a *central axis* of social relations which cannot be subsumed under
> or reduced to some broader category or conception. (1986, 61-62).

Race, in this thinking, is irreducible to other axes, like sex, class, or
nationality, each of which have sets, matrices even, of discursive relations that constitute social, cultural and political relations. It is a tremendously important category to contest and to understand as fundamental because it makes possible the lens through which we view
bodies. Linda Alcoff pushes this thinking by saying that our racial
identities constitute "bodily experience, subjectivity, judgment and
epistemic relationships" (2006, 183). None exists outside of or beyond
the purview of that gaze and way of producing knowledge of, by, for
and through race.

This very tension—race as a contested term, as a central site for inquiry—that Omi and Winant point to in their 1986 work is mirrored in and confounded by how writing center, composition and English studies have struggled to address it along with other identity politics. In her 1999 work, "'Our Little Secret': A History of Writing Centers, Pre-and Post-Open Admissions," Beth Boquet traces the history of writing centers, noting that many emerged in the 1970s as a response to a flood of previously un-represented populations of students on college campuses. This historical moment is rich in significance, the very occasion when civil rights, the New Left, student protest, anti-Vietnam war, and women's and gay liberation activism reached an apex of radicalism and challenge to institutional and social hegemony and control, as Johnson's Great Society programs failed to deliver substantial, sustainable change. Throughout society, anti-poverty programs combated generational hardship, from urban cores to Appalachia and southern rural communities, and the vestiges of Jim Crow segregation gave way to expanded "white flight" to suburbs throughout the nation. In the academy, people of color and working-class folk found greater access to higher education, but institutions struggled to understand their learning needs and styles, to develop processes to help these students accrue the educational capital required to be successful, or to challenge whether existing conventions fit the new realities on campus. In composition and writing center studies, the role of race, historically, has been embedded in debates over vernaculars and whether and how to teach to "codes of power," "code-switching," or "code-meshing." Carmen Kynard (2007) studies this history and its key figures, particularly in relation to the Students' Right to Their Own Language movement within the Conference on College Composition and Communication. She argues that Lisa Delpit (1995), who many in the field have championed for advocating direct instruction on the written and rhetorical codes used by those in the majority, problematically advances a pedagogy rooted in integrating black students into a middle-class cultural elite without reference to their "home" cultures and subsequent impact on literacies to which they have access. Instead, Kynard advocates critical awareness of students' literacy experiences and demands at home and school. Rather than exclusively focusing on such lower-order concerns as syntactical and lexical correctness, Kynard advances a pedagogy rooted in genuine understanding of students' learning experiences, better knowing how their "culture, history, or linguistic repertoire" impact on learning standard English vernaculars (374). Sound teaching and learning, she believes, places race as a central axis for discovery that struggles over language and race and makes possible different sets of knowledge and vice versa.

The importance of Kynard's 2007 work comes in the pedagogy it reflects and the value it offers for leveraging the multiple literacies that we all possess for learning in diffuse contexts. Just as important, it values—rather than marginalizes—the identities and communities that students bring with them, each of which themselves have linguistic, rhetorical, and symbolic protocol that learners can tap and bridge to other domains. This social negotiation enables us all to understand and explore how identity, but race in particular, signifies and makes possible a wide range of possibilities, as Alcoff anticipated, that are encoded on/through our bodies, our ways of knowing and doing, and the relationships we build with worlds near and far. Too often in our classrooms and writing centers, such awareness—that home and school aren't in opposition, but are mutually supporting reservoirs—is bracketed as irrelevant or a distraction. That message is ultimately self-destructive to learners and ourselves. Rather than foster the notion that a person's relationship between home and school be severed, we should instead create occasions for helping people understand when, where, and how home is appropriate for reaching different audiences in various contexts. While we must all integrate with the larger world and imagine social actors whose own experiences parallel and diverge from our own, we never compartmentalize our multiple experiences, selves and identities to any good end. In the coming sections, I turn to that negotiation and question an uncomplicated assumption of mainstream (white) ways of signifying our identities, and I advocate that we empower students to make strategic decisions about whether they accommodate, oppose, or subvert conventions around racialized discourse patterns.

ERASING AND MUTING RACE

When we talk about race in the context of writing centers, staff can become reticent to engage the conversation. Such ambivalence is rooted in the difficulty of approaching the subject, especially when participants, myself included, come from entrenched positions of privilege and power, or unlikely as it may seem, are from marginalized positions, and have little awareness of their exteriority. Conversations about the structural and institutional nature of race are viewed through a prism of what's gained from "making it an issue" when there's no clear benefit. I've heard white colleagues anxious about talk of race—of owning our culpability and benefits from institutional racism—who see it as an exercise of public self-flagellation, a performance without any tangible pragmatic outcome. What, they wonder, is the utility of owning a personal relationship with race and racism? What's the end of inventorying and testifying to privilege over other people? Others doubt the efficacy of writing centers as sites for launching social justice work in general or as spaces for critical dialogue on race: Why, they ask, must such charged discussions begin in sites often lacking in the political capital to effect change in something so systemic?

Each of these positions is indeed a plausible counter-weight to visions, admittedly utopian, of social change in academy. For the "why us" standpoint, the issue shouldn't be an either/or proposition, that race is either about individuals' culpability in institutional, systemic dynamics or about the structural physics of social relations that operate above and beyond individuals. The real issue is understanding that our everyday practices reify larger, more abstract forces in play, and that making change involves critical consciousness-making. We are, in other words, culpable in the social forces around us and have an obligation to speak into, reflect on, and disrupt them when appropriate. I advocate what Antonio Gramsci (1971) called "organic intellectualism," a sort of pedagogy rooted in enabling people to call into question the conditions that make possible their own oppression or domination (in the case of people operating from privileged standpoints). In composition studies, this thinking has been most widely taken up by followers of Paulo Friere (2000). Wherever the teaching of writing happens, the practice is embedded in dialogue where teachers/consultants encourage students to "problem-pose" ways of thinking and expression, that through critical engagement they will find a path to intellectual emancipation, at best, or greater voice and agency in communication, at minimum. In that latter sense, problem-posing presents a social justice pedagogy that's relatively hegemonic and oppositional in writing centers, even as many practitioners seek to resist understanding the activism implicit in their everyday routines. Writing centers, unique crossroads of students, faculty and institutional culture, are sites where organic difference can be made, even if tentative, ill-conceived, and halting. This intellectual labor is just as central to teaching in other contexts, where critical dialogue doesn't only lead to greater engagement and active learning, but creates possibilities for taking up content in more meaningful, sustainable, and resonant ways for instructors and students alike.

Racial identity politics involves dynamics where marked bodies, those of people of color, come to signify with an excess of codes, a comprehensive set of meanings, the absence of which, simultaneously, confers membership in discourse communities of unmarked bodies, populations with historical privilege and domination in institutional cultures. In practice, students of color and their use of language offer symbolic capital that's rendered as non-transferable to many academic rhetorical contexts by the majority.[10] Such language signifies, when it's refused or denied access, linguistic and rhetorical practices long established and inscribed onto people of color, typically from urban or southern rural communities and named as Black or African American English Vernacular (BEV or AAEV). Often there's a class dimension to the vernacular since middle- and upper-class people of color often present codes consistent (or compatable) with dominant/white use of language and rhetoric in those contexts, while working-class people of color often don't have equitable access to institutional structures (schools, cultural experiences) that would provide opportunities to learn "codes of power" or ways of transferring such symbolic capital, as Kynard (2007) might support, between literacy traditions. Language use and rhetorical strategies clearly have cultural referents rooted in communities bounded by shared identity (see Gilyard 1991, Smitherman 1977, Kynard 2007), but it's also evident that linguistic politics have material implications, assuming, of course, that individuals seek to break from or move into discourse communities that privilege one code over another. Speaking standard English *can* result in access to positions—jobs, institutions, culture—where that code is hegemonic and a taken-for-granted condition of entrée, but I'm not convinced talking the talk evacuates more residual or structural racism that renders most of dominant society tremendously segregated.[11] I push this point because I'm

---

10.   My use of symbolic capital here references Pierre Bourdieu's (1977, 1984, 1991) work. He argues symbolic capital is the elemental form of capital at the heart of other expressions—political, cultural, economic, social, etc.—around which fields and wider habitus are constituted and structured.

11.   In my lifetime, African Americans' earning power has rarely surpassed sixty percent of what white people make annually (See http://www.cbsnews.com/stories/2006/11/14/national/main2179601.shtml, census.gov, or Bureau of Labor Statistics, 2006). Only Latinos make less than Black Americans, while Asian Americans typically earn more than the white majority.

not convinced that teachers and learners often understand that choices and options exist between acquiring, adopting, adapting, and refusing the linguistic and rhetorical traditions of dominant culture. The pedagogical imperative is to foster awareness of the practices that render dominant or hegemonic discourse (their syntax, lexicon, rhetoric, etc.) as transparent and natural, appearing and existing without question, politics or implications; whereas other discourse practices representing any other identity formation are viewed as adjuncts, vernaculars or dialects that are somehow branches of the center. It goes without questioning that standard English and academic prose aren't themselves vernaculars, granted privileged ways of expression.

Not going forth into that dynamic—not to understand and critically engage hegemonic practices, whether conventions of interaction or language use—represents an attempt to erase identity at the center and the inscription of it elsewhere, on the linguistic and rhetorical practices of people of color. This move is tantamount to what James McBride (2006) remembered about his mother's explanation of her racial identity in *The Color of Water*. Growing up as a black man in Brooklyn's Red Hook section, McBride would, along with his siblings, ask his white mother about her race, the answer to which she carefully evaded. To her, she lacked race. The notion of white folks not signifying race seems, at first, like a dodging move in response to a difficult question, yet it captures a historical (half) truth, that people of color are historically raced and signified, while white people aren't in the same way. Of course, as a consequence of racing (and marginalizing) minorities (and remember, Omi and Winant (1986) argue this is a universal phenomenon), the majority is signified itself, if only in discursive opposition to them. White people come to have meaning in relation to people of color. Race, in this sense, cannot be understood in our cultural practices without exploring structuring oppositions: Whites cannot exist without the constellation of other racial identities, just as class, sexuality, gender, and nationality are also dependent upon the same unending set of juxtapositions. Defaulting to the hegemonic is posited as stepping out of identity politics, creating a vacuum where a neutral discussion of language can somehow be engaged without reference to historic, contextual, and rhetorical need.

Kenji Yoshino (2007) would refer to those defaulting moments as occasions when people of color are pressured to cover, to assimilate white norms of performing in the public domain. Yoshino, a Yale law

professor, explains the concept in legal terms, but it has wider reso-
nance. He argues anti-discrimination law distinguishes between immutable and mutable traits of identity. Immutable elements, traits that
cannot be changed like race, ethnicity, and sex, have legal protection
because they operate as forms of difference from the majority that people don't decide to invoke or assume, whereas mutable traits, cultural
expressions of identity that a person "chooses" to signify, can be regulated in such public contexts (130-131). Mutable elements can involve
everything from hair style and dress to mannerisms and language use
and create the basis for everyday—and legal—forms of discrimination.
Yoshino invokes Eric Liu's writing on the model minority to explain the
pressures people of color face:

> Liu stresses his "yellow skin and yellow ancestors"—he has not passed or
> converted. Yet he believes. . .covering behaviors have transformed him.
> Observing that "some are born white, others achieve whiteness, still others
> have whiteness thrust upon them," he says he has become "white by accla-
> mation." That metamorphosis is also internal. Liu says that insofar as he has
> moved "away from the periphery and toward the center of American life,"
> he has "become white inside." (1999, 125)

Yoshino reproduces a list from Liu's memoir, *The Accidental Asian*, that
details his "white" behaviors that include media, fashion, cultural, and
community elements, most of which could also be interpreted as middle-class behaviors. While American society has grown to tolerate racial
pluralism—what Yoshino would call *being* a racial or ethnic identity—
there remains deep ambivalence about *doing* it. In other words, it's fine
to be African, Latino, or Asian American so long as one isn't *too* African,
Latino, or Asian. The degree to which a person of color plays into that
protocol signals their complicity in covering their identity.

Covering is both a means and an ends that has a commonplace
and problematic existence in most writing centers and composition
classrooms, including my own. Students of color come to the writing
center, often with a surface expectation that tutors "fix" their papers,
with an underlying desire to cleanse their prose of markers of vernacular English and to adopt language use that sounds white or consistent
with the more amorphous "Standard Written English" championed
throughout the academy (I'll speak to the unique elements of this
pressure to "code-switch" for multi-lingual writers in a later chapter).
Whatever relationship they may have with standard English away from

school, savvy students learn the premium placed on its usage and the real consequences for refusing it, while less attuned peers are eventually told to write less like they speak and even later to speak less like they do at home. While "progressive" professors might grant permission to speak from authentic experiences, few tolerate or make space, real or rhetorical, for authentic language use, even make room for dialogue about the protocols attendant to discourse communities across the academy. Student voice might be championed as a means for engagement, relevance, and pathos, but being "real" or "true" works only inasmuch as it doesn't threaten the supremacy of dominant modes of expression. Tutors themselves are in vexing positions, as students of color themselves or not, because they are often quite proximate to the demands their clients face: Tutors personally know the demands of instructors since their jobs as such are predicated on pedagogical experience, if not quasi-expertise, with collaborative learning, itself a register of an ability to bridge teaching and learning. Writing centers, then, have a tacit assimilationist contract with the populations they serve: Covering, a performative logic of assimilation, involves sets of codes and ways of signifying to the expected terms of majority; and tutoring involves mentoring one toward acquisition of those rules of conduct—linguistic, rhetorical, or even behavioral. The question, the moral dilemma for tutors and students alike, is the degree to which they problem-pose that social contract, making space to realize its very arbitrariness and, regardless, power.

The temptation to default to the majority, to cover oneself in the trappings of white hegemony, provides an explanation for why students might privilege white tutors over those of color. Although thoroughly racist, students might logically reason that the most efficient way to acquire "codes of power" is to seek those who might seem to purvey them the best, tutors whose bodies at least signify their proximity to the majority. Ironically, in the very scenario that leads this chapter, Allia possessed much more privileged educational capital than any other available tutor in that writing center. She was in graduate school as a returning adult student having long ago completed an undergraduate degree at an elite east coast liberal arts college, working for years as a corporate trainer, and raising children. Of anyone available to this student, Allia was quite possibly the best suited to offer the rules and codes of dominant expression in American higher education. Of course, the student had no way of knowing that background before meeting Allia, and I'm not sure that owning such capital would ensure a tutor is effective. On another level, the student might have been registering another cultural assumption about race in teaching and learning. She might have thought, based on prior experience, that white tutors might be more likely to correct or fix her writing as opposed to an African American or any other tutor of color who might be known to make students work for their learning, to make clients active rather than passive participants in a session. In baiting Allia, the student was working toward a win-win scenario: If Allia caved to racism, she might be tempted to fix the student's paper rather than contest her, and if Allia passed the student on to someone else, she was more likely to get someone who would also do it, just "fix" her paper.

As troubling as I find that scenario for the tutor and the student and doubly so if the roles were reversed (and the tutor was tracking or profiling the student), I'm more worried by a response that might deny the role of race there. Because it is so invisible and hence structural and institutional, the quotidian experience of race and racism is less akin to what Allia experienced and more like the experiences that Geller, et al (2007) write about in *The Everyday Writing Center: A Community of Practice*, or that Villanueva (2003) describes in his *Cross-Talk* essay. Geller and her co-authors share the narrative of an African American woman who worked in one of their writing centers. She frequently got stopped upon entering the space and asked with whom she had an appointment. The student quit the writing center after she brought her son one day and a tutor commented that he'd make a great basketball player one day (87-88). The embedded assumptions about people of color not being figures who could be tutors, or narrow perceptions of life possibilities for black men, aren't original or terribly unique. At my writing center in Queens, young tutors of color have the same experiences at our registration desk, either with a new consultant acting as a receptionist or being relatively new among our community of consultants. But I've also heard younger-looking faculty get stopped and questioned by the same inexperienced people at our reception checkpoint. Whether the roots of the interaction are racism or unfamiliarity with who's who, the point remains the same: The tension between one's intent and reception is difficult to negotiate. These two situations remind me of a flashpoint in one of my graduate courses when a white graduate student, who by day directs a learning center and teaches basic writing courses, expressed frustration at the prose error her students, mainly people of color, were displaying. Her frustration was couched in a language of elitism and superiority that worked to Other her students who were already so ("these people can't even write a complete sentence"). However her frustration, as authentic, real, and genuine as it was intended, a call for help, was still racially tinged in a way that no white person can express without also invoking the cumulative history of institutional racism that her students' experiences with education likely index. Another student, one of a handful of students of color in our doctoral program, called this student out for the racialized discourse and the poverty of her pedagogy, suggesting that she had no business working with basic writers in this context. I've heard both of these rhetorical positions over and over in writing centers and at conferences over the years. It's a sort of discursive distancing where people are faulted for lacking certain educational capital, yet they are denied roots or strategies to overcome that gulf. This conflict testifies to the need for more, not less, dialogue among people in this class. That same Othering discourse is commonplace in writing centers, where first-generation students, especially when such students are of color, come in proximity to students, staff and faculty who don't understand, or don't have the tools to cope with the linguistic and material differences between themselves and clients. Such conversations shouldn't be censured; rather, processes and techniques need to be leveraged to make for safe and productive difficult dialogues.

There's even greater complexity in how race gets played out in writing centers. On the one hand, the need for multiculturalism, of which including people of color is a huge part, creates an inclusive space. But, on the other hand, conversation plays an important role regardless of what the face of the center is—there needs to be dialogue that's genuinely transactional, not about banking for any perspective or essentialist way of being, but dialogue that's a genuine exploration of difference and similarity, about same and other. The work doesn't stop with inclusion; it extends to developing mechanisms for mutual learning. To me, that's at the heart of a story Villanueva (2003) writes about in "On the Rhetoric and Precedents of Racism" in which he describes an explosive department meeting held to discuss dynamics that lead graduate students toward feeling as if they're pressured to don white masks in order to succeed in the program. The students, Villanueva shares, feel that race is treated as ancillary to curriculum as opposed to integral to it (836-837). One student argues about the difference between speaking and being heard, of being understood, internalized, and integrated. Hearing, and all that goes along with it, requires a level of performed reciprocity; interlocutors have to respond in ways that signify and name understanding or ongoing questioning. Greeting those moments with silence or not providing space for conversation to even happen connotes an environment just as closed and unwelcoming as any explicitly racialized or segregated space, thus making silencing a policing mechanism, a filibustering by static—or by white noise. I wonder, though, what about the writing center, where silence dominates, where no difficult dialogues, as one of my colleagues names them, happen. What does it mean to *be* silent as opposed to greeting moments *with* silence?

That sense speaks to the dynamics at play in the second scenario with which this chapter led. What does it mean to staff a center in inclusive ways, to do it with a select population of "model minorities," tutors who, without question, have adopted codes and discursive practices of the majority, and for all intents and purposes seem to identify with the cultural majority? What does it mean to be an interloper in that environment? To confess, those have been my writing centers, and each has had more than its share of "problem" tutors and "problem" students who both refused, regardless of whether they've been self-aware of that refusal, to wrap themselves up in the protocol and other unwritten codes of assimilation of the spaces. The material consequences can be harsh: ostracization at best, being marginalized and subject to greater scrutiny (as my partner says, "The nail that sticks out, gets hammered down."); or missed opportunities for voluntary collaboration and mentoring. On the flipside, for those who act as "team-players," the rewards range from inclusion to possibilities for academic enrichment and perks (collaboration on research projects, networking and special mentoring, etc.). I wonder now whether those students were truly problem students or tutors, individuals who just couldn't adhere to those writing centers' codes of conduct, implied or not; or whether the writing centers were enacting a pedagogy of covering, a *de facto* learning and teaching environment that privileged assimilation and that made resistance futile, if not untenable. My greatest fear, in writing centers where the cultural inertia is toward a sort of multicultural assimilation, is that the outliers are taught a dubious lesson: Everyone is welcome so long as challenge and doubting are silent. In effect, silencing becomes a *de rigueur* mode of operation.

FOREGROUNDING AND SUBVERTING RACE

In the everyday practice of writing centers and composition classrooms, race is invoked as an issue of linguistic and rhetorical assimilation or as evidence of a need for multicultural initiatives. Accommodation mutes the charge that racial identity politics can bring to learning and teaching and makes race a trait that needs to be neutralized, rather than a set of practices for which recognizing difference is prized and generative. When conversation turns to race in the writing center, so much of the talk gets framed in terms of an unending series of binaries that I just don't see as productive. People are pressured to uncritically adopt academic English in tension with racially and ethnically coded speech and writing patterns (among others) that are perfectly appropriate and relevant in a variety of rhetorical contexts and genres. In essence, the face that is proffered in writing centers is one that too often uncritically accepts dominant performativity. As Jacqueline Jones Royster (1996) puts it, authentic voice isn't just a matter for vernaculars or languages that have dominance away from school; all language is authentic, whether uttered in the academy or beyond. Yet such utopias are illusive in the everyday grind of learning and mentoring in writing centers and beyond. Although putting a public face forward that conforms to racialized standards of discourse usage is the default pedagogical goal and outcome, covering isn't the only option to which people from the margins have access. I propose they may also elect to assume oppositional and subversive positions in relation to the center. An oppositional standpoint, to borrow from the rhetoric of social movements scholarship, might involve a rejection of institutional and social structure, advocacy of fundamental, systemic change, and use of non-standard codes (Cathcart 1983). Stuart Hall (1993) defines opposition in similar terms: Recognizing the reception and circulation of codes and meaning in direct contrast to dominant ideological formation. Further, Malcolm X (1965, Cited in Grant 1996) and Molefi Asante (1987) each have advocated oppositional forms of consciousness, critiquing Western thinking as inherently Eurocentric to the exclusion of Asian and African philosophical and rhetorical traditions. To be oppositional, then, in the context of a writing center would likely be an untenable enterprise for people of color who are students or tutors. The collaborative nature of the dynamic of meeting students where they are, of understanding that tutors aren't necessarily spokespeople for larger institutional bodies and structures, creates a contact zone not entirely neutral, but also not entirely safe or risky for everyone and everything involved.

More typically, the moment for opposition comes in relational dynamics and while helping students negotiate their linguistic rights. Returning again to both scenarios that I led off the chapter with, I'm reminded of Allia's conflict with her student. An oppositional response would have involved directly protesting the student's action and demanding, understandably, an institutional response to her racism. Student life codes of conduct, particularly those that require a sort of decorum or common criteria for behavior, likely would have given her cover. More likely, and just as plausible, would have been Allia "going off" on the student, speaking out vociferously, even driving the student out of the space. More discretely, she could have sought out an administrator, a colleague, or someone else who could take over the session, in effect withdrawing from the situation and the symbolic, verbal abuse it was entailing. In the second scenario, the burden of action falls again on the object of tension, the person being raced in an oppositional way. Here, being thrust into a separatist position comes as consequence of *not* doing something, of not conforming or assimilating.

What feels more tenable to me, a position that enables everyone in a writing center to participate in advancing them as spaces for social justice, is one rooted in a notion of subversion. Cal Logue (1981) argues that a subversive position might appear as assimilationist, involving what on the surface might be interpreted as a tacit acceptance of institutional protocols and rituals of the wider system, but it actually involves manipulating discourse and populations in ways that advance individual needs while undermining the status quo. Logue believes a subversive approach involves rhetorical disguise and readiness as well as the use of language in coded ways that inform insiders (or confederates) and manipulate those in positions of dominance. He initially used this framework to deconstruct slave rhetoric when they spoke (and sometimes wrote) from positions where they had no practical choice between outright assimilation and opposition. They lacked the power to pick from those two positions because being truly oppositional had the direct consequence of violence and death. Students or tutors of color obviously don't face the same threats, but the material consequences of refusing, particularly in the context of education, are still nonetheless real. Can people of color, in effect, realistically take on a separatist approach to academic communities when they can't influence or bracket hegemonic rules and conventions of communication and practice that impact on material success, particularly in a society that places a premium on undergraduate education as a pre-requisite for most entry-level professional, white collar (or service industry), and increasing numbers of blue collar trades? Getting good grades, succeeding, and advancing professionally can often be predicated on playing along with the rules of the game, even at times when one wants to resist.

Rhetorical readiness and disguise are intrinsic to the learning and mentoring practices of writing centers, and it's a cumulative sort of capital that also develops with life experience. Tutors can be cultural informants, as Grimm (1999) advocates, bridging their own experiences with learning the academic ropes and rituals, to novice students who are often still learning their own sea-legs, not knowing where, when, how and who to listen to and observe. Consuming cultural capital, or learning the rules of its acquisition, isn't about a slavish adherence to tradition; it's about knowing enough to undercut and challenge from a position of security. Understanding conventions or genres doesn't necessarily mean accepting them as natural or given. Rhetorical disguise would involve using dominant codes of language in expected ways, to speak or write in ways that might otherwise appear to be covering or assimilating to white standards of conduct. But lurking beneath the veneer of this accepted, hegemonic use of language would be a special use of code that either contains codes for confederates or manipulates one's opposition to turn attention to some common enemy. This latter sense is what Henry Louis Gates (1986) theorizes as signifyin', a technique common to African American cultural experience throughout history. All of this work is consistent with what effective writers do in any context, to consider an audience and to use understanding of it to guide development of an argument. Sound tutoring involves dialogue on and questioning about what students know about their audiences as well as the genres operative in courses. However, subversion comes into play when both tutors and students collaborate with one another about ways of leveraging personal experience in occasions where professors might not otherwise allow it; or when they work together in developing appropriate, respectful ways to question, even challenge, faculty to re-imagine or refine assignments, projects or readings. In sessions I have had with students, more often than not, they've never had occasion to talk about the various ways in their everyday lives that they switch between codes for different discourse communities, from work and friends to family and elders. We've talked about how they came to know how to switch or change up the way they use language. Even when the linguistic differences were minor compared to the amorphous expectations of academic English, just having the conversation was empowering in the face of what might otherwise be seen as mystifying. My goal, in these sorts of sessions, is to have students and tutors alike recognize that we all have multiple voices and codes to invoke for our rhetorical purposes, that we have the agency and responsibility to strategically use them, and that sustainable change comes from having them in circulation, forcing institutions and the academy to evolve and adapt.

PARTING THOUGHTS

The face of the writing center is crucial. Having a disjunction between those tutoring and being tutored can manifest in any number of ways. It can create a colonialist culture from which a local form of stratification can emerge, and it can create an experiential dissonance for those entering a discourse community. Then again, I've only ever taught or worked in writing centers in institutional contexts where first-generation students, working-class students, students of color, or some combination thereof, dominate the population being taught. I've been in contexts where experiential gulfs yawned between faculty and tutors and the student populations in their writing centers. In each case, the cultures were dysfunctional for a whole host of reasons, yet none of those problems were insurmountable had there been spaces for speaking and hearing one another and seeking out ways to collaborate on ways to make sustainable social justice work. How people move between margin and center, how to face the center or the margin, is about a fluid process and product, neither one nor the other. As the U.S. moves ever closer to racial and ethnic minorities being the numerical majority (a reality in most urban centers already), the question of margin and center and politics of moving between both becomes ever more complicated. As people of color negotiate center and margin—whether, even, to move between them—a simultaneous negotiation must happen for white people, for people like me, who also need to learn a new world in which their experiences, their languages, their ways of knowing aren't always the default positions. In reality, most people reading this book, in the near- to medium-term, will likely continue to be overwhelmingly white and privileged if they index the current demographic trends in the field, and to these readers, I must implore labor rooted in inventorying our privilege and to invest heavily in strategies that mark us when unmarked and to contest the insidious ways in which we silence and fail to hear, to see and to listen.

Kynard's (2007) work speaks into the long history and politics of composition studies struggling with its surface politics and deeper lived practices at the intersection of students' right to their own language and institutional pedagogies of domination. Learning to write in a college classroom involves a negotiation of disciplinary and universal academic genres and rhetorics, but acculturation doesn't happen in a vacuum apart from the wider social and cultural practices that have historically made them possible. Our conventions signify who we are, and battles over them are charged with the identity politics always already operative in our society. Teachers, tutors, and students too often face a Faustian bargain: Acquire the keys to the kingdom, enter, and flourish, but you must leave your baggage, your socio-cultural heritage at the gates. But the academy has forever changed in the last thirty years as access to education has democratized. The face at the center doesn't necessarily have to be white, yet a multicultural one that lacks a range of linguistic referents isn't fundamentally an improvement. Instead, we must advocate multiple literacies—of home, vocation, passion, and publics—as a matrix of communicative possibilities that *everyone* must have facility with and a fully conscious repertoire to articulate them to audiences. Our being and doing race feeds the complexity and rich potential of learning and teaching, and should not be positioned as a set of variables to be overcome and mitigated. As central as race is to who we are, rendering it transparent or seeking to dissipate its role eliminates rich potential for expression and critical thinking. To empower students means giving them agency and opportunity to interact with all worlds possible through a range of terms and devices.

INTERCHAPTER 2

Rochell Isaac, former writing consultant, current doctoral student in African American Studies, Temple University

The one thing that my tutoring experience has taught me is that the lack of confidence surrounding the act of writing often centers on matters of agency. Short of ESL and other debilitating issues, the struggle to write centers around our (in)ability to process and evaluate (critical thinking), our (in)ability to express opinion with clarity, and/or our (in)ability to own our viewpoints/opinions. Of course, those requirements call for some measure of self-reflectivity. My tutees and later my students all seemed to shy away from locating themselves on an issue. It was as if the elephant in the room, the silent question being asked of me was, "What right do I have to an opinion on the matter of X?" This was followed by the not so silent, "Who could possibly think that I'm smart enough to evaluate X?" At those moments, I became supportive. "Yes you can," I'd interject somewhere in those sessions. Now I wished I'd been more open. It might have been more helpful to share how much of a fraud I sometimes think I am.

What I love most about this response is its subversive quality. As an African American woman, Rochell created a response that avoids directly engaging an earlier draft of this chapter. After my nagging and begging her to produce the comments, Rochell's thoughts aren't immediately about race, at least on the surface, and are instead about her everyday experiences today as a teacher. The response also speaks to a reality of identity that readers and I need to be attuned to: identity politics aren't totalizing to our experiences; who we are doesn't always already occupy what we do and strive for. What she couldn't have known was that all of my other former African American consultants who aren't already featured in this chapter also declined to contribute to this dialogue, and not with an active, "Hell no, I'm not doing that!" More often than not, they declined passively. Time intervened and their lives became occupied with other matters. Both Rochell's response and those of the others got me thinking about how the request was problematic on a whole host of levels. I wonder whether the response rate would have changed had I made a space for her and them to decide which chapters they could react to and on what terms. Instead, here and throughout, I sought out, in my best—and worst—well-meaning-liberal sort of way, people who seemed to fit the chapters' focus, positioning them as spokespeople or proxies for a way thinking and knowing. In theory, I knew no one person could stand in for a collective, even when the intent was to make representation more democractic and inclusive, yet in practice I still reverted to presuming that someone in Rochell's position had some transcendent view or trumping wisdom for the dynamics of race. In the end, the request wasn't reasonable or appropriate; she should have had the right to enter into this dialogue where and how she chose to.

* * *

Cameron McLinden, former writing consultant, St. John's University; graduate student in English, Brooklyn College (CUNY)

As a tutor, as well as simply a student interested in academia, I felt the pressures of conforming to the standard that is highlighted in this chapter, even though I am white. I grew up in the American South playing basketball and living in lower income communities; incidentally that placed me in a culture of the Southern black world. In college I found myself wearing baggy clothes and a backwards hat, hip-hop banging from my ipod, and speaking with a distinct representation of the culture in which I was raised. The attitude of academia and the writing center that hit me, in no specific way, told me I was out of place, needed to release the drawl in my voice, change my clothes, and essentially "act my skin color." It happened. I left much of the culture in which I found conviction for the "more proper" white culture I never got to know as closely as some now assume. The biggest place I found this pressure was in actual sessions – while peers who were raised in similar cultures embraced my tutoring more, those who were raised closer to the "proper white standard" at first had a look that seemed to show they thought they were on an episode of Candid Camera. I never confronted it directly, I always let my authority over writing do the talking, but it gradually pushed me away from what made me individual.

In what Cameron writes here, I hear echoes of experiences at the borderlands of class and race in the U.S. The pressure he felt but lacked the language to articulate speaks to the socio-cultural identity of someone working class, the focus of a subsequent chapter. But Cameron also speaks into an affiliation with an African American community back home that signifies as a culture both separate and aligned with his own in the South. I suspect the disjunction for his white middle-class peers here in the northeast at St. John's has as much to do with the remnants of redlining segregation as it does with economic differences and with the ways those privileges get mapped onto everyday experiences. In the South, working-class people, regardless of race, are more likely to live in close proximity to one another and come to know each other's cultures, not that familiarity has dissipated deep-seated racism and racialized oppression. In the larger urban centers of the northeast, migration patterns over the last fifty years, the ones that made the suburbs possible, reflect a pattern of "white flight." Federal, housing development, and mortgage policies encouraged first-generation middle-class Caucasians to purchase homesteads far from city-centers, usually to the exclusion of African American and other racial minorities.[12] As metropolises became more racially concentrated and polarized, the employment stock shifted as well, particularly as manufacturing disappeared. The result of these shifts was a concentration of poverty commingled with racial segregation, often leaving society to equate urban poverty with race. While they have become linked, the antecedents to this material reality aren't often explored; instead, a rhetoric of meritocracy justifies the suburban "utopia" and more recent gentrification and repatriation of cities by ex-pats of outer rings of metropolitan living.

That pressure Cameron felt to act white, to perform his whiteness, is a powerful insight to me because it represents an important move, as Frankie Condon (2007) would no doubt support, to inventory his own racial identity and the practices that make it possible and enforce our wider system of and discourses of privilege around racial identities. I also like that Cameron names a practice that permeates writing center and composition classroom practice—the circulation and normalization of codes of English that reflect racial as well as other hierarchies. To be "right proper" (white) in the academy can often mean learning to change the way we signify, in language, through our bodies, by our adornment. And each movement brings along with it a certain loss and injury, especially when people aren't allowed a space to negotiate the privileging of one discourse practice, to speak into it or to mourn its loss. If we don't enable that processing, in conferences or workshops, we risk re-enacting, re-enforcing the damage to voice and sense of agency, and undoing all our work to free up individuals from cognitive and social restraints to move toward unfettered expression (before it's ultimately adapted to genres and audiences). I wonder how we can make greater time and space for this decompressing without also being patronizing or unproductive.

* * *

---

12. For more background on redlining, see Nicholas Lehman's 1992 *Promised Land*, or Kenneth Jackson's 1987 *Crabgrass Frontier*.

Jennifer Fontanez, former writing consultant, undergraduate and Master's student, St. John's University

I recall one day in the writing center an African American student came in to work on a donor thank you letter. During our brainstorming session he very bluntly shared with me that the reason he believes that he is receiving this scholarship was "'cause he was black" and he "shoulda gotten more dinero" and "I should know what he's talkin' about." I asked him to elaborate and explain his responses. He responded by stating, "you should know what I'm talking about...I mean aren't you Spanish or Asian or some shit like that?" I was initially very annoyed that he would even think of using his race as an apparatus to obtain funding and that he was completely ungrateful for the donations. I then became even more aggravated that in an abstract way he related to me because in his eyes I was classified as a minority of some sort and so we must have shared some common experience. The student's assumptions were incorrect about how I identified. I was appalled at how he was using his identity to his advantage (even though I showed no sign of disapproval or approval) and I thought that he was a bit arrogant in the way he approached identity and used it to his benefit.

After reflecting on this session I realized that I, too, use identity in a way that would give me an advantage. My non-position or refusal to neither confirm nor deny is my way to gain advantage. I can morph my identity depending on my situation, surroundings, and audience. White tutees usually don't question my credentials because there are few concrete indicators that I might be different or the Other. Minority students often gravitate to me; they can identify with me because they assume we share a common identity or experience. Highlighting my heritage roots when it is beneficial and being silent when situations are uncertain helps me be a universal consultant.

My own identity will never be constant; it will always be in flux. Although I am first generation in the U.S., I not only identify with being Hispanic, but I can also identify with the dominant culture of my surroundings. This is not because I have mixed blood in my veins (I am a 100% Puerto Rican), but rather because I quickly learned the expectations of the dominant culture, instead of resisting it. I am in no way, shape, or form advocating for assimilation or for people to deny their roots; having a general understanding of expectations can give people the ability to move fluidly between two very different worlds. For me, it has allowed me to connect with people from all identities, thus making me more accessible.

I'm intrigued by the transition in Jennifer's feelings from visceral offense to a reasoned comfort with her positioning. What's lurks as a tension is the conflict she must feel on some level as a Latina whose identity has been assimilated into the mainstream (white) culture and society. The conflict becomes legible, for me, when Jennifer was surprised that an African American student would feel an immediate affiliation with her as a person of color, and when she didn't feel reciprocity with him. The reaction suggests Jennifer didn't see her identity as marginal/oppositional as he did, even as she recognized him in that role (as other). In the moment when Jennifer feels frustration with his apparent lack of gratitude for the scholarship he had received and for which he was being made to write a letter of appreciation to the donor, she best expresses the tension and gulf between her experiences with racialized marginalization. To Jennifer, this student's refusal to play along with the institutional process ran against the grain of her greater willingness to be compliant or accommodating to it. Her response also represents an important insight for the negotiation of the racial and other cultural assumptions in relation to institutional demands in writing centers and composition classrooms. How do we make possible venues for students to play along with, resist, and even subvert larger institutional practices, possibilities that no doubt lead to greater student agency and engagement? Like Cameron, Jennifer learned to play along with forces probably too big to challenge on her own, yet I wonder how we can tap into or better respect/honor students who find the rituals, as her client did, dubious at best. Must students always assimilate as Jennifer has done? What other possibilities can we present them that don't reduce the choices to "take it or leave it"? I'm also drawn to wanting to know more about how she works reconcile her strong identity as Hispanic with her life in the academy. Clearly, as Jennifer mentions, students are drawn to her because they suspect or assume she'll have empathy for their journeys. In spite of her stated assimilation, her ethnic identity remains strong, yet it feels bracketed for her everyday experience as a student, tutor and teacher. I wonder when Jennifer feels her ethnicity and when it informs and influences the empathy and pedagogy she uses with students.

3

FACING CLASS IN THE WRITING CENTER

Scene 1: David comes out of one of New York City's working-class Latino communities. He is very soft-spoken and tremendously self-conscious about his literacy problems. David talks to Elena, an honors undergraduate student, about his experiences avoiding gang life in his neighborhood. He sees college as a vehicle for leaving parts of his home life, yet the world he faces at college often is just as daunting and discouraging as the one he seeks to avoid at home. A subway ride connects his two worlds, yet that train ride holds them simultaneously in tension with one another. David brings his difficulty with reading comprehension and writing issues to the writing center, and his ability to concentrate on school is undermined by needing to work full-time. Although he struggles with academic texts, David talks about his love of reading and writing. However, when sessions turn to his composition texts, Elena speaks about her frustration at the plodding progress they make. David and Elena take a month of conferences to convince him to revise ideas before "fixing" grammar. She wins David over only after his professor compliments his prose and also encourages him to reconsider his argument. Initially he takes that news as a devastating indictment of his ability as a writer.

Scene 2: Toward the end of semester, Dane, a senior English major, first-generation college student and Italian American, comes to my office to talk about his future and career. He is excited that I have encouraged him to pursue graduate study, and he has also begun to think about becoming a New York City teaching fellow. But he is carrying a huge debt load coming out of our private institution, and he is worried about getting a job and providing for his girlfriend. So he wants to know, what do I think about him taking the civil service exam to become a sanitation worker? Starting pay is $40-something thousand per year.

In the last chapter, I wrote about the face of race in writing center identity politics. As these scenarios suggest, the discussion here turns to economic class, but it's hard to imagine class cleaved from other aspects of who we are since they are so intertwined with one another. In both cases, these young men work to negotiate a complicated set of social relations that predicate social mobility on education or specialized training, as Julie Lindquist (2002) would argue. My reaction to Dane indicates that not all routes to social mobility and economic security are viewed by people in positions of privilege equally, yet for him the ability to provide for his partner is more compelling than accruing the means to distinguish himself in other ways. Dane's relationship to meritocracy—to success and self-improvement—doesn't need to signify markers, at this point in his life at least, that differentiate himself from his working-class roots on Staten Island. Complicating matters even more, if someone like David pursues the promise of education and self-improvement, he faces a future that might distance himself from a strong ethnic community that provides a sense of belonging and attachment that may very likely be missing in any gentrified world he could inhabit. In sessions with his tutor, his use of language in college writing was framed in paradoxical terms: As David sought greater academic success, his vernacular was shameful to him; yet as his use of English in college classes grew better, he felt drawn away from his community back in Sunset Park, a working-class community of Latinos, whites, and Asian-Americans in Brooklyn.

In writing centers everywhere, tutors and clients like Dane and David are common, though how we acknowledge and contend with their existence, roles, and needs varies widely. First-generation students, academics, and administrators represent nearly three generations of formerly excluded people now gaining wide access to education. This shift was, in part, the product of post-World War II education policy, Great Society desegregation programs of the 1960s, and student protest movements of the early 1970s. Never before and nowhere else have so many had such great opportunity for education, even though financing for it has never been remotely equitable. Yet suspicion and doubt have been constant companions to this institutional democratization of teaching and learning. As access has grown, so too has the suspicion of these new faces: "Are they college material?" "Will they fit in?" Meanwhile, they themselves battle self-doubt and insecurity: "I'm an imposter;" "Maybe I'm not cut out for this life." Advocates of "maintaining" standards fear the prestige of college education will be soiled, its gatekeeping role to greater earning power and job security diminished and downgraded, slipping ever further into the horizon, like a

mirage, with undergraduate education no longer the de facto creden-
tial for most entry-level, middle-class employment in the U.S. With the
relative value and caché of college education unclear, high school education, beyond college preparatory curricula, today offers little to leverage for, except minimal credentials for vocational training. According
to the Bureau of Labor Statistics (2006), today only advanced degrees
correlate with generational class-changing earning power. Racial and
economic stratification in American education is worse now than at any
time during Jim Crow segregation (Kozol 2005).

It's no surprise, then, that students like Dane and David, products
of class-coded education, doubt their abilities and promise or worse, to
me, don't know what could be; if a person is never mentored or encouraged to aspire for any possibility, to embrace any dream, it shouldn't
be surprising that the alternative, just getting by or sustaining oneself,
becomes a life passion. Admittedly, this mindset is patronizing and
says a great deal about my own criticism of and cynicism about people
whose values, drive, and personal satisfaction come from other sources,
not necessarily from the workplace. It also says just as much about my
own lifetime of tussling with my parents who toiled at hourly-wage
jobs, who left work at work, but never seemed happy or fulfilled by it,
and who to this day wonder whether the academic labor I do is *really*
work. To them, work was a means to an end, providing a decent home
and food, yet I always got the sense they wanted something else, to
do something more; but being poor and having kids and a mortgage
superseded everything else. I wonder how many of my own students are
at college to create the possibility for the life my parents have had, one
not predicated on ever-escalating needs for consumption or happiness,
but one centered on being fulfilled and content. At institutions like St.
John's, where first-generation students dominate the undergraduate
population, understanding the inherent contradictions and tensions
of their pursuit of education is critical, but we also need to deeply
consider our own belief systems and educational experiences and the
ways they depart from and dovetail with those of our student populations, whether they have family histories with college education or not.
My tutors work daily with students who don't know why they're in college and what they eventually want to do; that's not so remarkable or
unusual for younger, less mature students. If anything, that lack of purpose can represent an exploratory stage en route to a sound, genuine,
sustainable professional plan. Instead, these students have been more

striking for their intensely focused learning and career plans as early undergraduates. On closer examination, pragmatism guides these students' orientation toward college. Their thinking represents less of a concern for intellectual development or personal satisfaction and more of a drive for vocational training that will ensure a stable income. Still that voice in my head whispers, wondering how many aspiring pharmacists harbor dreams of being philosophers, how many accountants wish to create poetry, how many biologists ache to be graphic artists. Connie, my secretary at our Staten Island campus, ever the realist and foil to my mischief-making, shakes her head when she catches me inviting students to indulge their dream majors or to experiment with classes that don't have an immediate impact on their careers, often saying later, "How many artists does the world need? How's this kid going to pay her student loans?"

Too often, being working class in the academy is neither a romantic Hollywood moment nor a source of gut-busting laughter. There's little nostalgia for *Working Girl*, *Billy Elliot*, or even *Roseanne*. More frequently, people who share my economic roots are propelled by institutional dynamics toward shame and regret. Everyday teaching and learning encourages people to shed this skin and adorn themselves in the trappings, affect and rhetoric of another world, one that assures material security even if psychic damage lingers unresolved. To better understand these dynamics, this chapter first focuses on the wider theoretical roots of the identity politics of class in writing centers, ways of understanding that are circulated widely in composition and English studies as well as in the broader humanities and social sciences. With that shared discourse in mind, I then focus on the ways writing centers and composition classrooms can play into the practices that paper over the performative difference of economic background in students' rhetorical and linguistic choices. In tension with these unreflective practices that normalize middle-class ways of expression, I wrap up this chapter by exploring occasions where students can be empowered to foreground or subvert their class positioning through writing center practice, pedagogical insights that have tremendous relevance in wider learning contexts.

THEORIZING CLASS AND THE WRITING CENTER

This book makes the assumption that many readers may not understand that they themselves possess multiple identities, ways of knowing that require naming and exploring, and that complicate their received meanings in relation to those self-constructed, let alone even contested expressions of Others. The collective identities and communities that form in relation to economic realities—those related to how much we make but also how we consume culture and signify ourselves in relation to those patterns—signify, to me, our class positions. Just as we never step outside or get beyond race, class is, quite simply, ubiquitous. To understand what it might mean to cover, oppose or subvert the practices of class-based identities in the writing centers, it's necessary to have a common grounding in the historical roots of cultural studies and post-modern criticism, contemporary intellectual movements that take class identity as central fronts for understanding the operation of society and communities. Patrick Brantlinger (1990) frames the historical roots of academic interest in class in a conventional way with it emerging in Britain and becoming intertwined in similar intellectual currents in the U.S. For the Americans, a humanities crisis grew in the late 1960s as students came to see coursework increasingly irrelevant to their own experiences and needs, and professors came to view the humanities as intellectually dead. From the left, there was a desire to challenge the rising corporatization of and industrial ties in the academy. To what degree, leftists pondered, had the missions of colleges and universities shifted to mainly servicing the labor, research, and development needs of government and corporations? As colleges democratized access, broadened their curricula and exploded canon, Brantlinger notes, conservatives mounted a challenge as well, questioning the intellectual rigor and sophistication of college education as its face and curricula changed.

But there were deeper divisions beyond 1960s radicalism and transformation that presaged the arrival of cultural studies and postmodern criticism. Coming out of World War II, intellectuals reflected on its lessons and began to understand the power of culture but also the threat to humanity that its manipulation posed. The Holocaust was a case study in mass culture and its potential to steer wide swaths of populations to inhumane ends. Though the world promised, "Never again," the Cold War, McCarthyism, the nuclear arms race, assaults on the environment and one regional military conflict after another signaled continued humanitarian threats, if not the potential for repeated genocide, even species annihilation. Beyond these global threats, critics also began to realize that the promise of capitalism was giving way to a reality of entrenched class positions and conflict, reflected as much in the diminishing rate and possibility for mobility and shifting between them as by cultural practices that alternately papered over or exploited them. In Britain, this critical awareness gets the greatest attention with Raymond Williams's 1983 interrogation of the meaning of culture and his expansion of it. Conversations began to shift from purely "high culture" artifacts and their significance—"the best of what's been thought and said"—to popular culture, examining how people made use of everyday texts to produce a shared, collective experience. In the humanities, this inaugurated an ongoing tension between champions of "great books" or *belle-lettres* and promoters of pop culture texts like film, contemporary music, and other unconventional "archival" material. Aside from attention to mass-consumed items and the impact of mass media, scholarship also appropriated anthropological and sociological methods of studying the exotic Other in remote developing countries and turned these methods inward, usually to working-class communities in industrial contexts, or to the self. Beyond Williams (1983), Richard Hoggart (1998) and Paul Willis (1981) produced powerful texts not only about working-class life and literacy, but also about the policing of them from beyond, by institutions working to maintain the status quo. To join the middle class and reap the economic, cultural and social privilege that goes along with that, Hoggart and Willis both suggest, working-class people are required to surrender their affiliation in all senses, symbolic and performative, to move "forward." Richard Rodriguez famously identified with Hoggart's concept of the "scholarship boy" in his memoir, *Hunger of Memory: The Education of Richard Rodriguez*. Such figures, as they achieve academic success, find themselves alienated, not quite embraced by those for whom intellectual life is "natural," but isolated, seen as separated from a community of practice whose aims and mission are increasingly at odds with what comes "natural" for the scholarship boy. As Julie Lindquist (2002) points out, people who might be named as working class likely don't understand themselves in those terms and probably wouldn't have a language that would capture the experience. By and large, people tend to identify with the default category of middle class, even if they possess no rational or visible connections to the signifier.

This attention to class and culture resuscitated a historical interest in the question of why fundamental economic shifts hadn't happened or driven wider change. Social and cultural critics wondered, in the face of growing class difference, of mobility becoming less—not more—likely for wide swaths of people, why they didn't mobilize for change? The consensus answer, like racism, is institutional and systemic. Louis Althusser (1971) argued that institutions operate to maintain a stable society and serve to hector people into subject positions, identities, in other words, that possess individual and collective ways of being. These positions and their social, cultural, economic and political values come to signify to themselves and others in hegemonic ways that maintain rather than challenge social order. Althusser pointed out that ideology was functioning smoothly when a cop or other institutional figure could call out, "Hey you!" and the right target would turn, performing their interpolation into their subject position. People, in other words, come to accept their positions as a natural course of events. Failure to improve one's lot in life signifies individual failure, never any broader institutional or social deficiency. Althusser believed institutions—schools, churches, the media, family, politics, etc.—worked mainly to discipline people and coax them to behave and believe in ways that seemed coherent and natural, even against their own material interests. His student, Michel Foucault (1977), produced later scholarship that advanced a deeper understanding of institutions and disciplinarity. He argued that institutions, from psychiatric facilities to schools, strove to generate information on individuals that they could then parlay as esoteric and generative of insight and expertise. The ability of disciplines to translate and interpret knowledge into truths about their subjects trumpeted their arrival and status as *real* sciences. These "soft" sciences, human and social, became linked to their "harder" cousins, proffering if not empirical truth, knowledge that they agreed was valid and reliable. Just as important, the knowledge they produced served wider social interests by developing, executing, and naturalizing mechanisms whereby people came to accept technologies of domination and subordination, the automatic functioning of power. People, under their influence, come to perform in expected ways, the product of institutions naturalizing their socialization through surveillance, knowing they'll be caught and corrected if they act outside of socially accepted roles.

Pierre Bourdieu (1977, 1984, 1991; 1992) takes Althusser's (1971) insights in another important direction, arguing that institutions and collective identity operate by complex hierarchies of capital, the combination or system of which he calls habitus. Complicating conventional notions of economic class as the primary means by which society is stratified, he explores how status involves much more than income or what other forms and amounts of property and assets they possess. How people make money and use it for consumption, and to what ends are just as important for insight. Bourdieu believes we actually struggle over wider sets of capital, many of which are directly related to how much economic capital we accrue, but some of which operate outside their influence, with hierarchies independent of monetary worth. He takes as examples the artist, craftsperson, teacher, and banker. An artist might have a great deal of cultural capital, but lack economic and political capital. A craftsperson, similar to the artist, might have a good deal of practical education capital and because of the person's trade, have significant earning power, but they might lack social standing. Likewise, a teacher might have middle-class standing because of her/his education, secure employment and earning power, but she/he might lack elite standing culturally, socially or politically; whereas the banker has tremendous capital across all fronts. In this sense, people might be economically middle class, but culturally working class. They might be politically and economically elite, but have little cultural value. To Bourdieu, fields—in their broadest terms, the economic, the social, the cultural, and the political—operate on the accumulation of power and status conferred through the capital that individuals and groups possess. Capital has complex sets of rules and protocol that themselves are context specific and expressed through symbolic capital that operates through language and the meaning attached to objects. Like chips players gather in a poker game, capital's worth comes with its sheer amount and the contexts in which we develop it. Everywhere from marginalized to dominant communities, capital operates to distinguish and stratify participants, but its transfer to other fields is always subject to their rules. Street cred doesn't signify beyond the street, gold coast or country club etiquette doesn't work outside its manicured lanes, and esoteric academic capital rarely passes muster outside its ivory towers.

   Bourdieu (1991) and Foucault (1972, 1977, 1978) represent important influences on postmodern and critical cultural studies trends in composition studies. Bourdieu's (1991) relevance to writing centers, in particular, comes in the awareness that people's use of symbolic capital signifies their membership and status in communities of practice. People never step outside of them and co-exist in multiple communities, each having their own literacies that can complement, confound or challenge one another. It's not a question of being deficient or lacking generally across fields, but one of recognizing that people need to *possess* and *use* symbolic capital according to its protocol, one that's always fluid and ready for change. The pedagogical challenge for tutors and students alike is to teach and learn the iterative and arbitrary nature of discourse communities, especially within the academy and its sub-specialties. But just as important is the need for awareness that understanding of one's own already existing capital, forms of literacy with which one has facility, can be leveraged or parlayed for others, and that's not to suggest we should surrender one for the other. Instead, having insight on one protocol (if not multiple versions) demysti-fies and facilitates learning and teaching others; transfer of learning becomes transactional, not linear. Foucault's (1977, 1978) work under-scores how this dynamic—of learning, decoding, and performing sym-bolic and cultural capital—lends itself to binary modes of operation, ways of using capital that are simultaneously normalized (accepted) and pathologized (rejected). He posits that the two positions are co-dependent upon and reinforce one another. This mutually-constitut-ing discursive practice has a daunting implication for those who hope to breach hierarchies and status regimes in discourse communities: In the instance when Other threatens same, when abnormal challenges normal, the privileged position works to reassert itself by shifting the rules of the game, rendering fields endlessly elastic and seemingly always under crisis, in need of policing and surveillance, lest standards and prestige fall. I'm not suggesting anyone abdicate working toward change or social justice, especially in our work to make the academy and writing centers more democratic, equitable spaces; rather, I'm advocating attention to the "reality" that institutions that we participate in are committed to and structured for manufacturing difference and policing it, just as we who mentor must work to counter and mitigate it.

It might be easy to look askance at the role colleges and universities play in normalizing the symbolic and cultural capital operative in their disciplines, working to exclude people who don't play according to their arbitrary rules, but that very logic is at play in every community or collective. Julie Lindquist (2002), in her ethnographic study of a work-ing-class bar, discovers a rich dynamic wherein people perform their identity, gaining street cred by acting and arguing rhetorically *within* the community, not by naming or using the vocabulary imposed from *without*. A similar sort of ethos is struggled over in the academy, in writ-ing centers specifically, when students and tutors alike must contend not just with disciplinary identities but the communities of practice that go along with them. They must also come to negotiate faces and performativity, although they often have little understanding of who they are, or of the implications of that knowledge, especially when those identities are marginal. Donna LeCourt (2006) conceptualizes this dynamic as a question of rendering class identities invisible. Working-class students come to view this self, she says, so readily disposable, so easy to bracket, that they likely have no ability to name or even recognize core traits, both cultural and physical, that distinguish them, ironically enough, quite legibly to everyone. LeCourt posits that colleges and universities play upon notions of class mobility and meritocracy, a social contract for improvement, yet they also offer themselves as institutions that transcend class even as their educational policies often reinforce and police difference. "Class difference," she notes, "through the maintenance of exclusionary discursive practices, reflects an identity that cannot even be discussed within academic discourse lest the institution's claim to classlessness be undercut" (LeCourt 2006,161). In this sense, then, facing the center is to mark the middle-class identity practices that are never interrogated and to help students and tutors alike come to name, even develop, a critical relationship to the ways we marginalize working-class experiences, even when we seek, justifiably, to transform them. As LeCourt herself acknowledges:

> The desire for economic security is literally quite real: Those without financial means are discounted, vilified, and held up to ridicule in our society. To be without money in our society is to be oppressed in the most structural of ways that literally put the body at risk: homelessness, unemployment, poverty, violence. (2006, 5)

She and I both share a profound commitment to empowering students, helping them achieve whatever level of material and symbolic security they seek (as we ourselves have done), yet we both value attention to the cumulative damage of lifetimes spent denigrating one's cultural roots as well as the need to discover and reclaim working-class identities. Part of that work involves creating spaces and opportunities for students and ourselves to explore and investigate, learning to know them as communities with rich cultural and rhetorical heritage.

Still another site for labor involves creating wider audiences for the insight this discussion of class and cultural studies provides. Tutors, writing center professionals, and teachers across the disciplines need to know not just their own identities as "classed individuals," people who carry with them numerous practices and socio-cultural assumptions about the economic positions we occupy. As leaders and mentors, we also must dig deeper into what makes these identities possible and sustained over time. We all need to understand the dynamics at play to curiously mask them, transform them, or imagine class doesn't exist. Instead, as actors in our spheres of influence, we see others with economic subject positions different from our own; we mark them through a range of personages, more often as "at risk," "remedial," or "first generation," than as "elite," "advanced," or "traditional." We get to those discourses through institutional practices that trace individuals, normalizing and naturalizing certain ways of doing and conferring and inscribing the capital they use in everyday life. The potential for activism and transformation through pedagogy exists in helping students and clients become aware of both the practices of domination (assimilating to the mainstream currents) and the possibilities for opposition and resistance, as the next sections will pose.

ERASING AND MUTING MARGINALIZED CLASS

In so many ways, what we're pressured to do in writing centers is to cleanse working-class students of their identities, to enable them to start reading and sounding like right-proper middle-class folks. If, as Susan Miller (1991) argues in the "Feminization of Composition," the role of teaching college writing is to potty train novice writers in the demands of college-level writing, then Lynn Bloom's (1996) characterization of first-year writing as an occasion for washing off the remnants of lower-class living is on target. Those first-generation students are a dirty lot: messy backgrounds, filthy ideas, sloppy organization, and soiled prose. It's a miracle more writing studies teachers or writing center tutors don't morph into Joan Crawford in *Mommie Dearest*, breaking out Comet in moments of exasperation and scrub, scrub, scrub, screaming in ecstasy, "Christina!!! Clean up this essay!" Setting aside all the Freudian implications of this widespread, albeit odd compulsion and obsession with the unclean, there's a paradox here operating through the movements to simultaneously erase and re-inscribe class-coded uses of language. As hyper-attuned as academics are to working-class rhetoric and vernacular, of outsiders in the midst, they also seek to eliminate it, telling students to adopt, without question, academic discourse practices that propose to be neutral. These default positions are anything but; by positing academic discourse as anything but *that*, the discourses that working-class students use, their language practices and community instantly signify as exterior, opposed to but also constituting academic language. As I said before, I'm not necessarily opposed to a common ground vernacular, even if it possesses a profoundly flawed historical lineage, complete with exclusionary and elitist politics, so long as we go forth understanding and teaching students to know its position as arbitrary, fluid, and subject to constant change. As any linguistic historian of English will confirm, the language is elastic and evolving, so for anyone to posit any common use of it as static is foolish; to teach any group of students, especially those who speak and write from marginalized positions, that in order to be successful they must surrender whatever Englishes they possess for some transitory "standard" version is wrong and unethical.

Writing centers and composition studies have a complicated relationship to the imperative to cover working-class identity. For people who espouse pedagogies ranging from expressivism to social construction, mentoring fosters voice, agency, and critical understanding of discourse communities and institutional practices. Across the continuum of expressive writing practice, I often see undergraduate projects in my writing center where students are being encouraged to express themselves and develop confidence and purpose with writing, to boldly share narratives they're burning to tell the world (without regard, I might add, to the extent of these enterprises' sheer narcissism or to whether the world is equipped and prepared to receive them). Another current compels students down a road of discovery of individual, collective, disciplinary, and/or institutional consciousness. At its core, this sort of curriculum is a vertiginous quest to deconstruct personal narratives and ideological interpolation even as students are pushed to assemble coherent arguments naming their marginality or privilege. This enterprise translates into a practice of proselytizing students toward hyper-consciousness of their fragmented identities, the shibboleth of which is their ease at naming them. For both of these curricula, disciplinary genres and conventions about prose (or shared approaches to inquiry, rhetoric and arrangement) are less compelling than an abiding faith in the impact of getting students writing, becoming confident self-reflective writers, and going forth engaged and purposeful. However, the academy persists in its mixed messages: It celebrates authentic voice and strong sense of mission, values that would seem to embrace a wide swath of vernaculars; yet the academy clings to static notions of rhetoric and presentation that can confound novice writers.

Bloom (1996) further unpacks these implicit middle-class values that college composition champions and that many writing centers often are complicit in enforcing. She names self-reliance, decorum, moderation, thrift, efficiency, orderliness, cleanliness, punctuality, delayed gratification, and critical thinking as hallmarks of middle-class sensibility that must be cultivated in "unwashed" students. Self-reliance centers on inculcating people with a sense that writing is a solitary enterprise even when many projects involve collaboration and workshopping (659). Decorum references the manners that middle-class writers ought to display like, as Freedman describes, respect, deference and appropriate formality (660, Cited in Bloom, 340-42). Respectability is the assumption that students should not display attitudes that transgress mainstream beliefs, whether radical leftist or conservative ideas (659). The goal is to always be polite. Connected with not offending any audience's sensibilities is the importance placed on moderation, to appreciate a reasonable range of perspectives on any given topic (661-662). Thrift and efficiency connect with both labor—working quickly—and financial mindsets—saving for a rainy day. They are also relevant to prose—eliminating excess and keeping it short and simple (662-663). Cleanliness indexes surface error, producing writing free of offenses to standard English, from spelling and punctuation to vocabulary and style (664-665). Composition also teaches the virtue of punctuality—getting work done on time and in sequence—and it services students for later writing in disciplines, planting seeds that will germinate later. ("You'll appreciate this experience when you're in that writing-intensive course in a couple years.") Finally, Bloom argues that teaching to critical thinking illustrates the independence and moderation that are cultivated in the other values. I would deduce from her argument that effective student writers who perform a middle-class ethos show great facility moving between intellectual positions of believing what they're taught and imagining possibilities for doubting, within reason.

Taking up Bloom's register of middle-class comp values makes me feel a little bit slimy. I like to imagine myself as being above stooping to such pedagogical bias, of being thoroughly implicated in teaching students to cover working-class identity and to foreground a purely middle-class mindset. It makes me think: "I'd never do that. My tutors would never encourage *that* kind of thinking about writing." But then again, I realize, of course, we all do it, all the time. Students come to us under pressure to "fix" their papers, to clean them of the filth of poor mechanics and style, having been told to stop writing like they speak, that their affect isn't appropriate for academic discourse. We never tell them, "Eh, don't worry about that. Your professor will get past all *that.*" In meeting students on their terrain, where they perceive their needs, we're compliant, never challenging students' expectations or their professors' edicts. We aim to please and go along, compliant, ignorant to the implications of what such work has for language or students' rights to negotiate their own understanding of English, adapting it to other communities or literacies. The writing centers that I've help direct more often than not struggled with the stigma that results from our willingness, ill-conceived or not, to fix students lack of proficiency with academic writing. As a consequence, these writing centers have drifted toward being or have become sites mainly for remediation, places where damaged or flawed writers go to get taken care of, where they learn to cover. Professors often play into stigma, referring only "deficient" students and telling others, "You don't really need that place." Yet in needing help, using it too much, students can still mark themselves as flawed and suspect in problematic ways, especially if their writing makes too much progress or development after working with a tutor. "Surely," colleagues have told me or their students, "this can't be original work. They've worked too closely with a tutor." In this complicated calculus, students ought to progress, get better, but not so much that they lose too much of their marginality. They ought to perform well, just not *too* well. Writing centers don't do enough to advocate and educate faculty in the range of literacies students have access to and their potential for transforming teaching and learning in the disciplines. Writing centers, as we will see in the final chapter of this book, concern themselves with covering well, being dutiful servants of institutional needs, training and retraining toward membership in academic discourse communities, often not advertising the wide range of students they work with, the full menu of possibilities beyond lower-order concerns we can address, and the recursive and iterative process through which that work proceeds.

Nancy Grimm (1999) reminds us that helping students acquire the markers of the cultural dominance—to talk the talk, to walk the walk, to cover—isn't necessarily a bad or flawed function of what writing centers do. Helping students learn and perform the codes of cultural dominance, the routines of discourse communities, isn't problematic. It can even be necessary when, once students are in college, refusing to do so has real material consequences such as doing poorly in a course, dropping grade averages, hurting chances for advanced study, or diminishing potential earning power. I opened the chapter with David and his struggles with college writing. Much of the frustration he encountered with his tutor (as I remember from debriefing conversations with her) was the realization that he lacked the codes to "sound right," to express himself in rhetorical and linguistic ways that enabled him to fit in; instead, at every juncture he was confronted with the knowledge, by way of grades and teacher comments and self-suspicion, that he was an outsider through and through. David's tutor was a thoroughly middle-class white woman who had transferred to my school from an elite liberal arts college. She performed the very all-American college affect that David sought to mirror. Watching them from my office was a curious ethnographic experience: From afar Eliza and David looked like an ad for Abercrombie and Fitch, Eliza more casual and effortless than David, whose performance of the college boy persona felt forced, too self-conscious, at times. It was in this sense that he represented a failure to negotiate the complex rules of class: that to assimilate or cover requires a profound internalization and performance; and that success is almost always fleeting. I eventually lost contact with David. I moved on to another institution, so I never knew whether he ever learned to cover. But when I think of those moments spent watching him, the power and hegemony of meritocracy scare me: How much damage is done, I wonder, to Davids out there in colleges and universities everywhere, who think they're just not working hard enough, that they're lacking as individuals, deficient somehow. Those people, I fear, walk away from higher education, not because they find viable alternatives for vocational and professional training, but because they can no longer bear the continued assault on their sense of character and ability.

Such violence goes on and accumulates its effects in an environment where it's not contested and challenged. The first step toward pushing back at that reality and creating a different space involves the sort of advocacy that consultants can do in writing centers on an everyday basis: affirming the familiar, scaffolding students' academic arguments with rhetoric and experience from outside where appropriate, and bridging their cultural capital to the context and constraints of writing assignments. Even outside the context of one-to-one sessions, activism can involve raising consciousness among faculty at large about the experiences of student writers and helping instructors come to know the learning needs and baggage students and faculty themselves bring to learning to write (and writing to learn). I suspect teachers mean well (just as novice tutors do) when they admonish writers who use class-coded language to "stop writing like you speak" (as if the voice in either context is neutral and absent of deeply political and ideological referents). Knowing the impact of those words on their audience is half the battle, but a fuller sensitivity can arise from faculty reflecting on their own journeys to academic discourse, however distant, however coded. The next steps, beyond acting as confederates who shepherd learners from one discourse to another, involve making people aware of the legitimacy and possibility of opposing and subverting the codes and practices of domination.

TOWARD FOREGROUNDING AND SUBVERTING THE FACE OF CLASS

At the Harry Van Arsdale Jr. Center for Labor Studies in New York City, students pursue education in a rather innovative way that doesn't implicitly require them to surrender their working-class identities.[13] The Van Arsdale Center works with people in the trades, usually non-traditional or returning adult students, and it combines undergraduate degrees with apprenticeships toward journeymen licenses. The program doesn't view students as transitioning from blue collar or trade work; instead, the center embraces the labor and work in which someone can take pride and build a consciousness, placing a premium on studying "work, workers and the 'working-class presence'- social, cultural, and institutional in an historical and a contemporary context" (http://www.esc.edu/labor). What's striking to me about this sort of program is the oppositional possibilities that it opens up, that literacy and language needn't be understood in relation to conventional academic pursuits or through fetishizing undergraduate or graduate education as a pathway for collective social and economic improvement. Instead this center values workers by using academic learning as a means for being better practitioners of trades as well as citizens more broadly. This work going on at the Van Arsdale Center and in different ways at schools like St. John's represents powerful potential for opposition that lurks in students' and tutors' identities, if only we could cultivate and enable them to express them. LeCourt (2006) takes up Tom Fox's 1990 research

---

13.   The Van Arsdale Center is part of SUNY's Empire State College system.

on his writing classes to signal a key point that despite the supposedly class-neutral environment of colleges, working-class students implicitly seek economic mobility, but *not* social mobility (162). These students often don't want to surrender their community identities, to break from neighborhoods and wider social networks to which they have intense ties and loyalty. Such pride and connection, even if not named or understood in class (or racial) terms, is powerful, and it begs for mechanisms that make them visible. In an institutional context that's purported to transcend class, marking it, wherever, however possible, is a profoundly oppositional act. They are, in essence, fundamentally resistant, working to resist being assimilated, even as they work toward a "cover" identity that provides for the material success they seek.

At St. John's, where forty percent of our admitted students must be in "very high need" of financial aid (at or below the federal poverty level), the economic mobility that college education promises, illusory or not, has the potential to transform individual lives and communities. I suspect we have legions of students who constantly juggle that affinity for home and neighborhood with the potential for a life and world somewhere beyond what their parents might have had, though they likely don't have a language for such experiences. Dane, the former tutor of mine I wrote about in the beginning of this chapter, is an example of someone seeking economic mobility, but not seeking to leave his community behind. He went on to become a New York City police officer, stationed the last I heard in the Flatbush section of Brooklyn. Dane was on the path to a secure job and stable life that he sought, and he wasn't trying to become someone he was uncomfortable being. When I now look back on those conversations focused on talking him into applying to graduate school, my vision was for him to become the sort of English teacher and professor who could reach students in ways profoundly different from some of my colleagues, as a role model who shared students' own cultural capital. What I hadn't thought about was that very experience of going to graduate school, of moving further away from neighborhood and community, would have fostered a greater sense of loss and estrangement. I would have been pushing Dane to assimilate to another world to which he held, at least at that time, no affinity.

In everyday tutoring, sessions could be spent raising consciousness, getting working-class students and tutors alike to foreground their experiences in every instance, or proselytizing about the virtue of owning or reclaiming one's identity. As Lindquist (2002) points out, that sort of activity is precisely the sort of naming and action that people don't do; rather, they perform in their everyday practices and community interaction. Ordinary interactions in writing centers involve establishing and building rapport with clients, coming to understand and empathize with one another, negotiating expectations, and setting an agenda. In the last chapter on race, I wrote about subversion involving an awareness of one's environment, a sort of street savvy applied to spaces of domination. Subversion also involves performing in ways that are consistent with the mainstream, in ways that disguise challenges or knowledge being shared among confederates. In working with students and helping them eliminate those tell-tale traits of working-class practice that Bloom (1996) alludes to, tutors lead students toward communities of practices, but they do it, especially when the tutors themselves are working-class, by parlaying shared experiences to new contexts, rhetorical occasions, and academic genres. I imagine someone saying, "Hey, I've been there. I know what you're going through." Even for students who don't share a common ground in terms of class, reflecting on and invoking their own experiences with marginality can mitigate the gulf just as much as making a discursive space for identity to be spoken about and problem-posed. The trick to pulling off that sort of conversation is honoring experience without the student coming to feel objectified or patronized.

In a recent graduate course on research methods, I mentored one of my students and former tutors in the very subversive ways that I'm advocating. Peter was struggling to come up with a topic for a semester-long project, and I had long ago read him as a working-class guy from suburban Long Island (his language and affect signified him), though I didn't think he had any self-awareness as such. The more I just talked with him, the more I learned, the more he told. He's the son of one of our campus public safety officers, himself a retired NYPD cop. While his dad and family had achieved sufficient economic mobility, they had left the old neighborhood in Queens, but had recreated it out on the island. In my relatively short life in New York City, I've come to know that police officers and firefighters alike joined the white flight in the 1970s and 1980s as suburban development and mortgage practices accelerated a temporary expatriation from the city (that trend has now reversed). The impact of this migration of newly economically secure but culturally working-class folks on the island was an oddly explicit segregation of the island along the route of the main expressway and northern and southern coastal shorelines. Working-class white folks populated communities and villages along the middle of the island, just far enough from the axis formed by Long Island Expressway so as to not hear its hum, but not too close to tony villages with water views. African Americans, by and large, were restricted to communities nearest the highway and closest to JFK airport's take-off and landing routes. These settlement patterns translated into Peter growing up with a Long Island sense of privilege (much of Queens and Brooklyn are signified as threatening urban blight, albeit thinly racially-charged in its encoding) but unaware that where and how he lived still signified him as working-class, dramatically different in self-presentation and style from peers who had grown up and attended wealthier school districts further out on the island or in elite communities near the coasts.

My knowledge of this economic and racial redlining of Long Island had only come from working with high school teachers throughout the island who spoke to vastly different experiences. In a tremendously wealthy district, instructors would tell me about the pressures they faced for their students to have high scores on SATs and AP exams, not just to ensure they got into "good" colleges (Ivy League or elite, selective small liberal arts colleges and universities), but also to maintain high property values. Their colleagues in less privileged districts spoke in the same ominous and earnest terms, except the codes had shifted. For students from working class schools, the anxiety was directed at students who "couldn't write," students who came from broken families with checkered histories, students who just needed the "right" templates to pass Regent's exams or do well enough on English Language Assessments to keep them from having to do summer school. With the distance and remove that I had as an outsider, I clearly could see that young people didn't automatically become less smart just because they lived on the wrong side of Route 25 or the Southern State Parkway. Obviously something was going on, something entirely consistent with what Jonathan Kozol (2002, 2005) has written about over and over again. Knowing Peter was the product of schooling on the "wrong side" of some highway on Long Island, I set him off reading Mike Rose's (2005) *Lives on the Boundary*, Jean Anyon's (1992) study of class-coded curriculum in New Jersey (not terribly dissimilar from the Island), and Kozol's *Savage Inequalities (1992)* and *Shame of a Nation (2005)*. Not surprisingly, Peter came back to me pissed off because I had asked him to approach these texts thinking about whether he recognized his learning experiences anywhere in them, fully knowing he would. I had worked to raise his consciousness, but the outcome of the work was still in progress. Peter was becoming self-aware, yet I wasn't sure whether he would handle the implications of that knowledge. Rather than just passively accepting his place in the social order, Peter now stood at the precipice of Hall's (1993) divide between being oppositional and subversive; he wasn't sure whether to reject or negotiate some place of security with it, but he was resolute that something in his head had shifted.

PARTING THOUGHTS

I don't have many stories to share of tutors and clients coming together to challenge the system, to "stick it to the man" (often a professor) from a position of relative safety. As someone fully implicated in the very system I might like to see students rage against or at least buck, I'm no longer in a position to daily witness routine subversion. Walking through the writing center, I do often hear students whispering to one another insider knowledge about how to navigate the waters of this or that professor, colleagues of mine whose arbitrary rules and regulations for essays range from the esoteric to the convoluted. Just as often, in their persona as peers whose expertise isn't necessarily content-related but based in understanding the cultural rules and protocol of academe, they act as Bourdieu (1984) would imagine: Explaining how to gather up chips and when to spend them. Tutors channel Foucault (1977), showing peers where a disciplining gaze comes from and how to act from a position of not being seen, to dupe the enforcers of normalization and perform the culturally pathological without getting caught. They are informants in the best organic, socially sustainable sorts of ways. As "impartial" advocates, my tutors quickly come to know they can't take sides for or against their peers, but they do learn to speak in guarded ways and careful cues that dodge being directive, weave around evaluation, and parry toward effective assessment in ways that enable their peers to do better without compromising their principles.

More often than not, I parlay the lessons of class identity politics that arise in the writing center to my own classrooms and when I'm working with faculty who seek out consultations. Students like David and Dane are a dime a dozen at the institutions where I've taught over the years, but the ones who are rife for consciousness raising are few and far between, making the syllabi for my courses and the discussions that crop up all the more strategic. I don't miss an opportunity to plant a seed or offer a question that challenges what superficially seems ordinary and customary. As powerful as those occasions are for my undergraduates who can find themselves questioning practices that had seemed natural, graduate students have also proven equally interpolated into unexamined class identities. On one occasion inviting a student to read Dalton Conley's (2001) *Honky* led him to finally reconcile with his own working-class roots and conflict with expression and being a part of the academy. In meetings with faculty across the disciplines, I speak, from time to time, about my own personal narrative as evidence of proximity to our students, and the gesture almost always results in colleagues having their own "coming out" confessions of working-class identity. Those talks inevitably lead to critical examination of assignments, syllabi, and pedagogy, discussions whose impact leads to small and large shifts for teachers and students alike. Such talk can also create a critical mass and confidence to push back at the unchallenged bias of privileged faculty, particularly when they seem insensitive or callused to the plight, needs, and assets working-class peers and colleagues bring to the academic and professional life.

As I mentioned earlier, I'm struck by the sheer diversity within our writing centers and our general stasis toward not engaging that diversity, however it appears and manifests itself. LeCourt (2006) confirms what wasn't surprising to me: Institutionally colleges and universities offer themselves up as domains that step beyond class. That professed blindness to differential experiences between students is an illusion that enables professors and administrators alike to carry on with the fiction that the playing field, if not equal, becomes so under our guidance, that we marshal the energy and forces to level everyone by the time they leave us as undergraduates. For those who refuse or can't be leveled, we think, "Well, they probably weren't meant for college anyway." The reality is, of course, quite different. The distance between margin and center, in economic terms, is wider and more fluid than ever. At colleges and universities nationwide, the middle class is quickly dissipating, receding back into the ranks of the working class, a move that I don't view as inherently tragic per se. It's an identity that requires reclaiming and celebration. Still, the material implications are nevertheless daunting: Fewer students have access to the loans and grants that enable enrollment at just the moment that employment opportunities that don't require college credentials become few and far between. The days of factory line work and stable manufacturing jobs have been swept into the dust bin of history; what remains are service sector jobs, the possibilities of which are daunting when factoring in lifetime labor. (For more, see Barbara Ehrenreich's 2002 *Nickel & Dimed* or 2005 *Bait and Switch*.)

INTERCHAPTER 3

Anna Rita Napoleone, former tutor

My first semester as a writing center tutor, I recall trying to hide my way of talking because I didn't tawk the tawk. What I came to realize is that many of those coming into the writing center tawked different and I loved it. One day, I had a Russian tutee (we were assigned tutees that would come for weekly appointments) come in and say she wanted to fix her grammar and I talked to her about process and that language acquisition takes a while. After all, I'd been in the country for over twenty years and I still had an accent but I did and I didn't realize that my accent was a classed accent. However, I knew how it translated within the classroom, on paper, and to some professors and it was frowned upon. I felt like David, ashamed, embarrassed but my talk, my tawk, was linked to greater things than school so in my shame and embarrassment there was a lot of anger. I started to discuss with the tutee that grammar isn't everything and that grammar is linked to bigger issues than just "getting it right" but she didn't want to hear that; she wanted a grade; I wanted a fight.

This tension between Anna Rita and her client speaks into many of the issues that arise in writing centers and composition classrooms around the politics of language, and also the subtle ways that class (or mitigating class) plays out in sessions. The underlying assumption here is that grammar and accent signify our class identities, even when we're not aware of them. Our codes and affect also perform many other aspects of who we are—our race, sex/gender, nationalities, etc. Here, I'm also interested in the relationship Anna Rita feels between this woman's ethnicity (she names her as Russian and likely, given the New York context, also an immigrant) and her class position. In this case, I suspect Anna Rita understandably turned toward advocating a critical awareness of the language enforced versus the language natural to one's voice. Her own early embarrassment, and journey to reclaim her code beyond the academy figured in Anna Rita's empathy toward her student, based on what she assumed was an experience they had in common. I wonder whether that concern was premature or reflected an agenda Anna Rita brought, a priori, to the session. Just as students have a right to their own languages, to channel Kynard (2007), Delpit (1995), and

Parks (1999), my gut tells me they also have a right to refuse critical consciousness or to come to it on their own terms. To question it differently, what are the conditions or contexts that make empathetic or critical intervention appropriate and which are less tenable? Under what circumstances does this sort of discussion transition from advocacy to proselytization? I suspect the tipping point comes from cues that a student or client might present that suggest frustration with or anxiety about admittedly arbitrary standards of language. Otherwise, I'm tempted to meet clients where they are, as opposed to where I'd like them to be. The experience provides a lesson for critical pedagogy that we've learned from the false debates of being directive or non-directive with students in writing centers; perhaps the real decision point involves not whether or not we should raise consciousness but whether or not the context lends itself to the sort of conversation a student can hear, internalize and act upon (at some point). Rather than push our students into fights that they haven't picked on their own, we are better served to enable them to choose battles that match their own agendas and sense of activism.

* * *

Kerri Mulqueen, Doctoral student and former writing center tutor at St. John's University, chairperson of the English department at Nazareth Regional HS (Brooklyn, NY)

Growing up the child of an Irish immigrant father and a first generation American mother, neither of whom had the opportunity to pursue higher education, I somehow always considered myself middle-class. It wasn't until I began my doctoral program that I really took stock of my personal history and realized that most of those around me had not grown up watching their parents work twelve hour swing shifts in the decidedly blue-collar jobs of, respectively, an emergency room nurse and a doorman/bartender/porter/superintendent. My parents were a part of the unionized labor work force and they enacted the working-class culture of only buying things they could pay for in full, working as much overtime as it would take to buy a home, pay the bills, and have gifts under the tree every Christmas. And always they pointed all four of their children toward college campuses with the clear message that it was those expanses of green grass and red brick that allowed one to move up in life.

In the last few years, I have come to realize that my constant drive to prove myself, to excel, to be recognized, has its roots in the story of my parents and my upbringing. There is a part of me that needs to justify my place in the academic world and there is a part of me still working to validate all the hours they worked, the tuition they strained to pay, and the encouragement they doled out to me to "read, read, read...."

Kerri's experience is common and shared by so many folks on St. John's campus and around the academy. I think of so many of her own peers whose experiences could easily share these pages with hers and mine, and I think of the canonical texts in cultural studies from folks like Paul Willis (1981) and Raymond Williams (1983) and those who have taken them up like Richard Rodriguez (1983) and Stuart Hall (1993). In composition studies, working-class voices further multiply as this last chapter suggests. Writing centers are critical sites where students like us can find a professional home and supporting place to learn and mentor one another. But just as important, our writing classrooms have an obligation to make a space for exploring and bridging the gulf between home and school as well as the challenges, opportunities, and losses that come along with movement between those places. Still, it's not enough to have occasions for expression; teachers and consultants alike need to consider when and how our pedagogies and work reinscribe differences and the guilt/shame/conflict that attends overcoming or bracketing them. Without such problem-posing, we're doomed to be repeat the history of William's and Rodriguez's "scholarship boy"—the one who can't go home again, but who can never feel quite secure in the academy either. We also have a duty to enable students to see that the dilemma of choosing between home and school is false because the inevitable consequence of that choice is giving short shrift to where we come from. How might we develop ways of growing that enable pride in one's roots, especially when our education takes us, in real material ways, away from them? How can we come to see and use our origins, their histories and places, when they aren't the ones typically normalized or venerated, as grounds on which to reflect and leverage, as central to how we learn, rather than as impediments?

4
FACING SEX AND GENDER IN THE WRITING CENTER

Scene 1: Kyle comes to my office in the early evening. The center has gotten quiet, so I initially think he's about to tell me he is closing up and heading home. Instead, he says he'd like my advice on a session he's currently having. Kyle's working with a male freshman who's writing an essay in which he's making what Kyle perceives as a homophobic argument in opposition to same-sex marriage or other gay-rights topics. Kyle wonders how he should handle the student. Before responding, I wonder why he has approached me? Is it because of my own identity as a relatively out, but not terribly vocal gay faculty member, or is it because he's genuinely interested in my perspective? Then again, Kyle, in the prior two years that I've worked with him, hasn't approached me before. Is it because I'm a safer figure to talk to in relation to this situation than his friends otherwise hanging out in the writing center? What does this situation suggest for the climate in the writing center?

Scene 2: An orthodox Jewish student gets banned from a writing center after he interacts abrasively with the women he encounters over a series of months: he commands them to correct his work, shouts at them when they refuse, and stares at their breasts. When male administrators and tutors interact with him, he is compliant and self-restrained. How typical is this sort of gendered relation? How does a writing center honor traditions tied to religion or culture while ensuring they don't confound commitment to diversity or a safe workplace and learning environment?

Just like race and class, our sex, our gender, and the politics attendant to them are ubiquitous in writing centers and to the people that circulate through them. These components of our identity are among the most legible on our bodies and the faces we present. They are also fraught with complication and the potential for misunderstanding. Wrongly reading one person's sex or presupposing values around gender and sexual expression presents minefields as well as opportunities for learning. Our postmodern society and culture make possible fluid codes that are paradoxical: invariably visible and hence public, but intensely private and difficult to challenge. Referencing moments when we check a sex box on some form or glance to a gendered ideograph, knowing and thinking, "That's me," Donna Haraway (1991), the renowned biologist/feminist/science fiction writer, argues such acts perform our socialization and—almost as importantly—our recognition of its operation in smooth and seamless ways. In checking ourselves, literally and symbolically, we give testimony to the hegemonic fashion by which sexuality and gender operate and also hint at the risk attendant to expressions that run counter to the dominant expressions. The automatic functioning of mainstream gender and sexual identity politics, the seemingly effortlessness of expressions that appear normal, even natural, of course, begs their very question. As we mark who we are, we signify the operation of social and cultural forces on us.

People's access to education and literacy is charged with politics and carries the weight of wider historical relations, all of which impact on their sense of agency and facility with writing for particular discourse communities, most often the academic. Our gender and sex are among those political and historical variables that cut through the scene of tutoring. For some, the point of entrée into this conversation vis-à-vis writing centers revolves around gendered notions of writing—that there are uniquely male, female, feminine or masculine ways of doing and learning it. While such insight has validity, it also can be essentialist and prescriptive, papering over the diversity of expression and eliminating possibility for dialogue about how gender and sex play out in everyday exchanges in conferences and beyond. Such notions about how we recognize and respond to gendered or sexualized interpersonal conflict or issues that exceed the text in writing centers make me nervous. I'm never entirely convinced about the degree to which people are even cognizant of the dynamics and imprint of their identities, in whatever way they are expressed and inscribed on bodies and interaction. My preference is to err on the side of consciousness-raising and problem-posing, to make a space for positing what we believe and challenging what might otherwise seem commonsense. In other words, I want to name and dialogue about the dynamics of gender and sexual face in writing centers. I've argued before in this book, and I'll do it again, recipes for "how to" are not so interesting to me as the questioning of "what makes possible" dynamics that might go unrecognized. I'm not positing a program for how we deal with issues of gender and sexuality when they arise in sessions. I'm not advancing a sense that sessions focused, for example, on high-order concerns need to follow any particular protocol read through a feminist or queer theory lens. Instead, I'm proposing that gender and sexuality make possible and intersect with other elements of our individual and collective identities, as writers, students, tutors, administrators, faculty, whatever. Gender and sexuality are central to who we are and provide a register of what's possible.

Unlike other chapters in this book, I approach this one feeling aspects of who I am foregrounded in my consciousness more than others. I feel and experience this face more intensely than others. My whiteness provides a level of everyday privilege that is so natural and smooth that I rarely question it. Only when race inserts itself into everyday life, as if somehow exterior to me, do I come to realize I am myself raced and benefit directly, tangibly, from that racing. The distance between my middle-class reality with its comfortable living wage and my working-class roots grows wider each year, yet student loans and rent remind me of the material "tax" people like me pay, that diminish our earning power and social mobility and keep us from moving easily toward "ownership class" existence. In those moments of clarity, I am acutely aware of my relative class privilege, even though I still hold the neurotic belief, one that many like me who have jumped class positions feel, that it's all temporary and fleeting, that my fraudulent existence as middle-class will be revealed and taken away at any time. Those voices, quite honestly, rarely shove other more pressing concerns aside in my thinking. Instead, it's my sexual identity as a gay man that confounds my standing; it challenges dominant codes of gender and sex and how they are performed on a day-to-day basis. My masculinity is often suspect—I'm never quite "one of the boys," but women in my professional life don't feel any necessary need to ally with me, no doubt the result of my own performed paternalism and sexism. A day rarely passes when gender identity politics don't assert themselves at the oddest of moments and in the strangest of ways. From speculation about the leadership hierarchy in our writing institute—who counts as "alpha males" (or their proxy female equivalents) and who doesn't—to the informal protocol (and violations of it) of how we deliberate and make decisions, gender is insinuated into assumptions and discourse practices. Even more, bodies themselves are sites on which a careful set of expectations are overlaid—women's bodies are subject to scrutiny (too much skin, too sensual, too informal), while men's rarely elicit such explicit questioning. Likewise, emotion and expression are embraced in prose, but allowed bodily performance only in very prescribed contexts and with only particular personae—the hysterical female, the fretting gay man, the angry person of color. Tension arises when affect and interpersonal interaction venture from polite casualness to intensity, rawness or vulnerability. It reveals a continuum of tolerance and latitude directly tied to conventional expressions of gender and sexuality that roughly parallel the hierarchies in place for race and class in our society. Coming to understand amorphous politics or the range of cultural assumptions about identity, gender in this context, presents another set of faces people must learn to manage, regardless of whether they are dominant, oppositional or subversive possibilities.

I write from the position of a writing center director in one of the more unusual contexts that a person can find her or himself. Around the country, many more women serve as directors and professional staffers than men, yet the directorship of the writing centers at St. John's is exclusively male. How that came to be is complete happenstance, but the role gender plays for us is rather vexing. The typically male privilege of leadership—"taking charge" and "running with the ball"—is challenged by our reality of a multi-campus writing center that requires coordination and collaboration. We boys can't just go off on our own. My benchmarks for writing center administration are contradictory and encoded with gender politics: I'm accustomed to writing centers where graduate students, disproportionately women, take on the lion's share of the day-to-day operations, or writing centers managed by an administrator aloof or removed from the usual hum of the center. Having the benefit of full-time associate directors on both of St. John's main campuses, I've repeatedly returned to wondering what role gender, even sexuality, plays in my struggle to be a better administrator leading two straight men: To what degree does my stubbornness or tendency to act unilaterally reflect weak leadership or a gendered approach? How does my need to nurture and cultivate relationships dovetail or challenge expectations of women and men? How do our struggles to work together as a cohesive team signify our inability as men to collaboratively problem-solve and manage a team, or the inability of straight men to rally behind a gay person? To what extent does being gay and out intersect with or complicate gender assumptions and tensions? Often I channel my dad and his life in the army. I think of its policy of "Don't ask, don't tell" toward homosexuals: As long as identity isn't disclosed, service members may serve, lest it impact on unit cohesion because, the thinking goes, straight men can't rally behind a homosexual leader. Although that mindset presumes so many linkages between sexuality and gender and leadership that are flawed and problematic, I'm left wondering if the policy could be on to something, especially in moments of self-doubt.

When I'm thinking about these sorts of questions, I quickly turn to popular usage of feminization. I first encountered the concept as an undergraduate in history courses where professors would talk about the face and feminization of poverty and education. In both cases, it signified an ominous turn, the intensification of a social problem ("That can't be good," I thought): the ranks of the poor becoming dominated by female-headed households, itself a code for the stigmatized welfare state. Likewise, feminized education meant an institution somehow had been overrun by women, an evidently problematic turn of events. Later I would discover feminism as a pedagogy, a process, a democratic mechanism, not anti-male but pro-collaboration and suspicious of unwarranted competition. From Susan Miller's (1991) work, I learned that this notion of feminization, particularly when it's invoked in composition studies, cuts any number of ways—one direction that held powerful, even utopian, possibilities of feminist theory re-imaging social space as more egalitarian, and other directions that served to marginalize and diminish the work of individuals, collectives and units. If, as Miller speculates, composition studies programs have become the potty trainers of novice writers' work, what must that bode for writing centers, frequently positioned as the sites for further, more intensive discursive remediation? Questions of gender are also complicated by discourses around sexuality. Just as the politics of feminism holds out the possibility for a society where masculinities and femininities don't index a person's worth or domination, it, along with critical race and class theories, makes possible a questioning of the place, function and implications of how our sexual personae and practices play out. Contemporary sexuality studies aren't just about making our society and culture safe for sexualities on the margins; this scholarship also studies the immediate and wider implications of organizing individual identities and social relations around practices defined by an ongoing and self-perpetuating struggle over what's normal.

Sex and gender play out in writing centers on an everyday basis in ways that are often very typical. Composition courses and other disciplinary subjects invite students to take on controversial subjects or issues that might appear to be unconventional. The first scene isn't terribly unusual today, even at a Catholic institution with a complicated historical relationship to the issue of sexuality. That Kyle took pause to question whether to help a student write what he viewed as a homophobic paper is progress; more typically, the tutor would just go forth, enabling, even fostering, such rhetoric. Still, the question of how we mentor oppressive discourse is one for local debate and ethics statements, though my centers have consistently advocated that tutors work from their positions of comfort and mentor students to consider how assumptions about audience (its composition and needs) reflect bias or require complication. More pressing to me are the deeper questions about the climate that has been created in the writing center. On one level, Kyle's comfort with approaching me represents a positioning of me as an object of safety, someone to whom posing questions on issues related to what Jonathon Alexander (2008) might call sexual literacy is non-threatening. Still, I wonder about the message for the student, regardless of whether he is pro- or anti-homophobic, and whether Kyle's reaction was tantamount to a sort of regulation of speech and writing. On another level, I wonder how we naturalize or contest sexual expression? To what degree was that performance— stepping out of a session to consult a director, enacting a kind of regulation, stifling even indirectly—impacting on how a client might approach the next occasion. Then again, as a point of process, my staff and I always mentor tutors to collaborate and reach out to others when in doubt, to model appropriate and productive information-seeking behavior. The moment, nevertheless, begs exploration of which occasions cause us to speak to the face and diversity of sexual expression, how we make it possible, and why we make the choices we do. More often than not, talk of sexuality is going to come up in essays or projects that students are writing for courses that force them to grapple with society's and their own attitudes and biases. The contemporary controversies around gender and sexuality are stock fodder for discussion because they are rife with arguments, counter-arguments, and meta-cognitive learning about every point on the road to discovering one's own rhetoric and the challenges to it. In the midst of every object lesson, however, are real students, tutors, administrators, and faculty alike, for whom learning isn't just an abstract possibility. Visible or not, self-aware or not, they are the referents whose presence cannot be quashed.

Connected to such moments of unexpected dialogue—surprising deliberations, disquieting exchanges—I'm reminded of the frequency with which sex plays out in writing centers. The ordinary practice typically revolves around peer tutors dating, breaking up, or setting friends up with others. It's *Days of Our Lives* or *The Real World* meets the writing center. Like any other workplace or public domain where people intersect with one another, romantic entanglements are bound to happen, frequently with problematic results that hopefully don't disrupt the ordinary operation of the unit or create an environment where mentoring and learning can't happen. The other scenario that I lead this chapter with might be specific to New York City where sizable orthodox religious communities are relatively common in the outer boroughs and suburbs where I direct(ed) writing centers. We've had Muslim students uncomfortable working with members of the opposite sex, whether Islamic or not, and we've also had Hasidim or other orthodox Jewish men refuse to work with women in my centers. In these contexts, it's a difficult negotiation of public and private, of the secular and the religious, of the faces that are possible and permitted, but it's also a moment where historical and theological marginalization of women impacts in very material ways. We've also had female tutors complain about culturally isolated men objectifying them in overt ways (e.g., ogling their breasts) that these men might not do at home because women in their communities dress or present themselves in veiled ways. The situation begs a complicated set of questions about whose burden it is to adapt or accommodate to whom and to what effect. Like the dynamics around sexuality, these moments of gender conflict are fraught with policy and political complications. I've tended to assent to these students' cultural needs (and biases), opting for compromise aimed at making the center's environment more comfortable for any population, yet leaving unchallenged the cultural tensions at the heart of the dynamic. Sometimes, discomfort is going to exist regardless, irresolvable. The situation also leaves me wondering about tipping points or thresholds I would allow a student or consultant to cross: Would I permit racially- or class-segregated tutoring? What about political beliefs? How would I respond to someone who refused to work with a member of a sexual minority?

This chapter next explores the socio-cultural history of gender and sex to provide a shared route into their discussion. Such background understands these elements as critical to who people are—everyone negotiates their gender and sexuality—and also underscores the social and contested quality of gender and sex. Our classrooms and writing centers, like any space where people interact, are terrains where individuals and groups must come to terms with (or are conscripted into) positions that dovetail with mainstream, dominant expectations or roles. But people also find themselves in search of resistant or subversive positions to assume, all parts of negotiations on which this chapter will focus. In the everyday work of conferences and mentoring, writing centers are central sites where this sort of activism is possible (and common), but learning spaces anywhere can take a cue from these dynamics and integrate them into pedagogy.

THEORIZING SEX, GENDER, SEXUALITY AND THE WRITING CENTER

Before turning further to the ways in which the gendered and sexual face of the center can be covered, oppositional and resistant, it's important to create a common ground in theories relevant to these variables. Like the explosion of activism in the 1950s and 1960s around the other identities that this text explores, gender and sexuality experienced similar ruptures that reverberated widely across the society. This era represented a culmination of changes that paralleled and riffed off those happening around other movements or in reaction to them. At the same time, the shifts in gender and sexuality had their own genealogy that's important to honor. When speaking of the shifting status of women, we have to complicate the picture and return to the industrial revolution that swept the U.S., changing it from an agrarian-based economy into an industrial powerhouse, and arguably lasting well into the late twentieth century. Coming out of the Civil War, a middle class began to take stronger root throughout the country, enabling re-invigorated notions of the public and private. In antebellum American society, middle-class women were firmly ensconced in the private domain of home; while men took on roles as symbolic patriarchs, women held sway over home and as time went on the domestic sphere extended outwards from the physical location of the home to schools and institutions of broader moral education. In a public arena where commerce and government were viewed as suspicious sites of activity where the base instincts and nature of men were realized, women were positioned as pure, moral counter-weights and mothers of the republic and its children, shepherding them toward virtue and righteousness. Women's rights re-appeared with high national profile in this context, leveraging the moral status of women in society as a way to their public citizenship and governmental participation. When national suffrage passed for women in 1920, the struggle was still over their symbolic role in society; the divide between public and private hadn't broken down in broad terms for those who were economically privileged. Working-class women and women of color of any class position, in contrast, weren't as policed or hemmed in by more elite notions of domesticity. Economic reality forced women of lesser economic means out into the public domain in search of paid labor. For women of color, primarily African Americans, their place in public was tenuous at best because it had been profoundly undermined by Jim Crow segregation. And where segregation wasn't the law of the land, everyday racism and marginalization made life in public always subject to careful negotiation, regardless of one's wealth.

Following the cultural renaissance and openness of the 1920s, the nation's experience with the Great Depression and Second World War further transformed and challenged the place of women (and men) in society, particularly with regard to notions of the private and public. The economic meltdown shattered familial relations in profound ways. With wide swaths of the nation experiencing dramatic unemployment rates, men were very often unable to care for families and frequently left them in search of work in other parts of the county. This began the nation's experience with poverty being concentrated in female-headed households, especially in urban areas, where public and private safety nets kept them from outright abject existences.[14] Once the war effort brought an end to the Depression, Victorian notions of the family couldn't re-assert themselves. Men, if able or possible, participated in military service. Those left behind joined the war effort that came to be dominated by women's labor. For the first time in national history, women across the board were mobilized and encouraged to leave the private domain

---

14. Prior economic downturns had happened when the society was still largely agrarian and subsistence living meant that families could at least survive without aid from others. It also helped that in those times, families had extended networks of mutual support, whether with extended relations or cross-generational support. If grandma and grandpa couldn't offer support, then aunts, uncles, cousins, brothers and sisters were around for aid. Moreover, families were also larger.

for public participation. It was framed as patriotic duty: the Mothers of the Republic were repackaged as Rosie the Riveters. At war's end, dominant ideology quickly shifted, and (middle-class) women were implored to return to their roots—to their homes. But at least two generations of women and men had come of age since the last vestiges of Victorian mythologizing of domesticity had given way to twentieth century economic and social realities. Having lived through economic depression and wartime, these people, often new arrivals to middle-class domesticity, had no benchmarks for social expectations of the moral propriety to come. Television (e.g., *Leave it to Beaver*) and moral education campaigns (e.g., *A Date with the Family*) served to casually instruct codes of proper suburban behavior and etiquette, even as the first media firestorms about delinquent youth, rock-and-roll music, and subversive culture underscored problems in paradise. Beginning with the 1950s and continuing throughout the early Cold War period, people faced intense pressure to embrace a middle-class ethos wrapped up in the sentiments of suburban life where the public and private were once again broadly managed and coerced. Women were supposed to shift the technological prowess that they had displayed in the war years to the home front, making way for men to take up their rightful place in industry and business but also enabling women to transfer their former "talents" to transforming the private domain. In effect, industrial specialists were retooled as domestic engineers. Women were supposed to apply the same gusto and verve to meal production and house cleaning that they had once put toward work on assembly lines or precision welding.

In the midst of all the domestic tranquility that was supposed to mark peacetime, movements were breaking out everywhere throughout the 1950s and 1960s, as D'Emilio and Freedman (1997) have chronicled. From the counter-culture movement of the beatniks on the coasts to the civil rights movement throughout the south and the student right's movement on college campuses throughout the nation, socio-cultural transformation and challenges to national (if not generational) hypocrisy were afoot in the midst of a wider zeitgeist for sameness. Although the 1950s are often remembered as halcyon days of sock hops and drive-ins, the conflict of the *West Side Story*'s Jets and Sharks and "duck and cover" were closer to reality. Throughout the New Left (SNCC, SCLC, CORE, SDS, the Black Panthers), most organizations were dominated by men who largely took for granted female activists who participated in the movement or ignored women's

issues as opportunities to complicate agendas or visions for social justice.[15] Women were widely active in New Left activism, yet few received
national attention or assumed high profile leadership positions. They
were viewed as supporting characters, roles secondary to the men
championing visible change. Although simmering throughout the
1950s, as Betty Friedan captured so well in her 1963 work, *The Feminine
Mystique*, women began to organize along three main routes in the
wake of the 1960s New Left activism. Liberal feminism sought to make
social and cultural change through mainstream political venues, most
prominently identified with the Equal Rights Amendment (ERA) that
sought to change the U.S. Constitution to guarantee equality. It also
had profound, long-lasting impact with Title IX that brought equity to
college sports and greater scholarship access for women, as well as with
anti-discrimination efforts of affirmative action policies at all levels of
governments and corporations. Cultural feminism was ostensibly an
oppositional movement, much like its racial analog, Black Power, in the
1970s, and advocated a complete break from gender oppression and
movement toward a utopian vision of a post-patriarchal society. A third
wave of feminism, socialist-feminism that emerged in the 1980s worked
to bridge sex/gender as a critical lens through which to view our identities as structured and structuring.

Paralleling the same tensions around the roles and status of women
and men in society—that the public domain was decidedly coded as a
masculine, male-dominated space and the private relatively exclusive
to female/feminine influence—possibilities for different sexual expression, beyond the confines for procreation and conventional family/
relational units, also emerged as economic and social shifts happened.
As agrarian families slipped away from being the primary economic
engines of society, people began to move to urban (and later suburban)
areas that offered varied or different living possibilities, and they also
began to find and explore same-sex romantic relationships in space
that made them more viable and safe. At the same time, social scientific disciplines were emerging and growing their knowledge of "devi-
ance" studies, juxtaposing and naming "abnormal" sex acts as personages, personalities, or identities. Before the late nineteenth century, all

---

15.   SNCC stands for the Student Nonviolent Coordinating Committee; SCLC, the
       Southern Christian Leadership Conference (of which Dr. Martin Luther King, Jr.,
       was the leader); CORE, the Congress for Racial Equality; and SDS, Students for a
       Democratic Society.

forms of non-procreative sex, whether or not with a same or opposite sex partner, was treated as more or less equivalent and equally problematic, but as the fields of anthropology, psychology and sociology grew, scientists worked to define sexual relationships, practices and identities. As knowledge grew about differences, they gained wider dissemination and notice. The more sexuality was studied, the greater the attention it got, the more society began to know of the possibilities, the more people came to understand these aspects of themselves, and the more they sought outlets and spaces to express it. The relative sex segregation of the Depression and war years led people to encounter sexual identity, often unintentionally aided by military and government screening attempts (in their attempt to root out homosexuals in their midst, both often ended up telegraphing it as a possibility that people hadn't otherwise had the ability to name or conceptualize). By the 1950s (even with its intense culture of conformity), gay people saw other movements organizing and moving for social change. While the gay community was far more tentative and nervous than other movements of the time, it mobilized for action and gained momentum. This activism reached a critical threshold in the late 1960s when activists followed the lead of other identity movements and began to take on an oppositional stance to mainstream oppression. Throughout the 1970s, gay power and its liberationist agenda gave way to what we might recognize today as a movement organized around equal rights and protection under local, state and federal laws, if not some degree of mainstream tolerance and acceptance.

In composition and writing center studies, the "social turn," as theorists like James Berlin (1996, 1997) and Lester Faigley (1992) have termed it, has internalized the intellectual, cultural, and social transformations of the last forty to fifty years. As with the other identity formations that earlier chapters have addressed, gender and sexual identity politics have come to be understood as critical factors impacting on the very possibility of claiming an identity and producing it in relation to communities. Elizabeth A. Flynn writes, "A feminist approach to composition studies would focus on questions of difference and dominance" (2003, 574). Similar to class and race identity politics, gender and sexuality in our society stratify and differentially position people, so, as Flynn suggests, the composition classroom with its critical exploration of self and agency (at least in many curricula) becomes a logical site to consider how masculinities, femininities, and sexuality interact and impact on individuals, communities, and society. Susan Jarratt (2001) extends the concept to include insight on how teaching writing enacts inclusion (or exclusion) in gendered terms as well as how our language use performs the same structuring dynamics of differentially positioning women and men. In connection to writing center conferences, Meg Woolbright summarizes the imperative as "teaching methods that are non-hierarchical, cooperative, interactive ventures between students and tutors talking about issues grounded in students' own experience" (2003, 18). The values that each of these women advocate are entirely consistent with a pedagogy rooted in building and fostering critical awareness of the structures and systems that produce divisions in society. Short of turning composition courses and writing centers into group therapy or unsolicited consciousness-raising sessions, which critics like Richard Fulkerson (2005) have argued against, sound use of this pedagogy fosters deep thinking, audience awareness, and student engagement, learning outcomes few would contest. If we accept, as Woolbright points out, that apathy and resistance are hallmarks of Millennial Generation students, then giving them tools by which to reclaim and foster their own sense of agency and influence over learning and self-reflection might be among our best offerings as a profession. Queer theory complements this agenda, not just by offering another lens by which to understand how society structures difference, but by advocating a "reading against the grain" pedagogy that, in the first instance, challenges and destabilizes hegemonic binaries and renders most as fluid, as positions on continua. In earlier work, I've argued that queer theory also "considers ways in which language and epistemology construct and constrain possibilities for (sexual) identity and their implications for public and private practices" (2005, 43).

To channel Michel Foucault (1977, 1978), then, gender and sexual practices, discursive and performative, represent opportunities to study their archeology and genealogy. While digging around these concepts tells us a good deal about moments in time (what Foucault (1977) names as an archeology), a genealogical tracing of their roots speaks into the historical emergence of a set of practices. The present day discourses and performances of gender and sexuality represent a culmination of shifts around the economic and cultural meaning of women and men in society, the range of masculinities and femininities possible (or permissible), and how all of these play out in whatever local context. How we do learning and teaching in classrooms and conferences intersects with a wide range of conventions. Looking into the everyday work of one-to-one tutoring represents a local and intense pedagogy that produces not just writers and the texts that capture their words; everyday writing center practice reflects the challenges and tensions with learning that can be (and must be) taken up elsewhere in the academy. Just as we can see students and tutors alike struggling with and against gender and sexuality, with practices that are received or carved out on their own, what we make and inscribe as normal or otherwise has tangible consequences for inclusive practice as well as for what too often goes forward as hegemonic and unquestioned. This chapter will next consider the practices that lead to and make possible assimilation, resistance, and subversion of gender and sexuality.

COVERING SEXUAL POLITICS IN THE WRITING CENTER

It's important to begin a conversation on gender and sexual politics by exploring the ways in which writing centers contribute to their covering or assimilation. By and large, writing centers foster collaborative, supporting, and empathetic environments and pedagogy. They strive to be safe spaces or contact zones where facial difference is generally celebrated. More often than not, these inclusive domains have disproportionate representation of women, as tutors or clients, a reality that confirms stereotypes of men's reluctance to seek help (and women's comfort doing it). This gendering of support and peer mentoring becomes all the more intense when a space doubly signifies as remedial, somewhere a person who is deficient goes. I'm not saying that in reality, women are any less reticent about deficiency or getting "fixed"; there's just more of a perceived social stigma that goes along with men seeking help, as if reaching out diminishes our masculinity. In this sense, the scenario with the orthodox man on whom I focus at the beginning of the chapter is more a fluke than not. Writing centers, as spaces whose feminization ought to precede them, become arenas where the support they provide and the cultural assumptions that go along with them present unfamiliar points of contact between people who might not otherwise be thrown together. Lauren Fitzgerald, who directs the writing center at Yeshiva University (a peer university and active force in the writing center community in New York City), has the completely opposite situation with a staff of peer tutors who are only men. Since the daytime undergraduate population is exclusively male, peer tutorials were same-sex experiences. Lauren once mentioned at a local meeting of writing center directors that unlike men in other situations who have to be coached in one-to-one tutoring's collaborative rituals of posing questions and dialoguing, these men didn't require training in those skills because they had come to her after spending their adolescence studying the Torah and Talmud in Hebrew school, where the very pedagogical practices writing centers value happen in a same-sex environment. Typically, novice tutors spend considerable time learning to collaborate, negotiate and grow relationships, oddly enough learning gendered ways of interacting that often run counter to their instincts, especially when they are men. Whenever I walk through one of my writing centers at St. John's, during what seem to be effective sessions, I'm almost always struck by how much the tutor is talking versus listening, by how active versus passive the student is. Too often, when sessions seem off track or problematic, even if students or tutors are unaware of it, it's the inability to recognize silences and embrace them that's the problem to me. In most cases, it's the guys who won't shut up, and the female clients who defer. It's in those moments I wonder to what degree, to what extent, my tutors reify people's gendered experiences with teaching and learning.

Our socialization in the dominant ways of expressing gender, even our sexualities, is how writing centers play a role in fostering assimilation or covering, even if it's never fully conscious in the training and practice we do. If we accept what Susan Miller (1991), Jarratt (2001) and others have told us, that academic discourse and the wider discursive practices of academy are gendered, privileging masculine forms of expression, then we would expect to see flashpoints all over sessions where students are encouraged to play into patriarchal norms. Eavesdropping on sessions will often reveal gender bias: Male tutors unable to allow silences to happen, to seize upon lulls to switch from questioning and problem-posing and move straight to offering up directive advice, a masculine need to fix things. These tentative insights confirm what Laurel Johnson Black (1998) found in *Between Talk and Teaching: Reconsidering the Writing Conference* a conversation analytic project that focused on writing conferences between composition instructors and their students. Even though this study wasn't looking at peer tutors per se but at interactions where the participants had greater power relations than typical in writing center contexts, the dynamics, as best as I can tell, and Black's insights have validity and relevance. She found significant performative gender differences between female and male students and teachers alike. Female students were more likely to be tentative, evasive, and cooperative, while their male counterparts acted with confidence and sought to dominate or contest interaction with teachers of either sex. Male teachers tended to interrupt women much more often than men and coax them toward shared positions through discourse markers that indicate they're in cahoots with one another. That sort of relationship-making didn't appear to happen when these men conferenced with male students; instead, by and large, dominance was ceded to male teachers, and the male students tended to resist more through silence and passive challenge. Though they didn't tend to use relational markers with either sex, female teachers acted like their male peers by controlling the direction and flow of talk. Black's study indicates that our pedagogy in sessions enforces and normalizes gendered ways of collaborating and interacting, but it also suggests where some roots of conflict might lie. What does it mean when either tutors or students don't perform in their gender prescribed or mainstream sorts of ways? How do we react? Do we make allowances to improvise, or do we have trickster tools to which we can reach?

By and large, I don't think writing centers have techniques and strategies to cope because this sort of pedagogical enforcing of gender happens in compulsory, hegemonic ways. The work of composition, whether in conventional classrooms or face-to-face sessions, almost never takes up reflection on the insidious ways in which learning to write normalizes gender as Black documents so well. It's an automatic functioning of domination that goes on unfettered in the background. As Black recalls about her own experience as an undergraduate:

> I realized that I didn't see myself as an active participant in such social and power relations (with teachers). Rather, I saw the traditional relation of teacher and student as "right" and "natural." Positioning myself within those structures, I willingly participated in my own domination, only occasionally and vaguely aware I was doing so. (Black 1998, 65)

Like Black, I look back on my own sessions and am a bit chagrined. In what ways did I enact male patterns of domination? How do I construct the students as gendered Others? Yet just in that moment of recognizing my own complicity in gendered teaching/learning binaries, I also begin to think about how I might perform at gendered cross-purposes by being a gay person. By being nurturing and allowing silences to happen, by deferring to where students wanted to take the session, by acting self-effacing to defuse my status as a proxy expert for academic writing, was I feminizing myself? To what degree was that problematic, and to what extent was that enacting gendered stereotypes around sexuality?

Oddly enough, in writing classes I've seen over the years, curricula often focus on self-awareness or critical consciousness of social, cultural, political, even economic forces at play. Students are coming to the awareness of their agency and voice or the social construction of their ways of thinking, doing and being, even while the pedagogy operative in their classrooms and conferences works to reinforce dominant rules of performativity. If the paradox of the composition classroom and writing center conference is stark, I wonder whether the disciplines do any better. I remember once debating gender politics and writing with a colleague in chemistry who took great pride in the neutral quality of writing lab reports in her field, or our male psychologist colleague who shared her sentiment and was a bit dismissive of what he called the humanities' compulsion toward fluff, emotion and confession. In that bracketing of gender, was the result really neutral? If the rhetorical style that made them recoil was so thoroughly gendered—feminine, in fact—what must the default position signify? Their thinking, not isolated I suspect, led me to concede that the disciplinary conventions and genres of modes, process, argument, mechanics and style may not be intrinsically gendered; rather, the values attached to communication performance and rhetoric don't step out of modes of signifying masculinity and femininity. A lab report doesn't seem gendered, and constructing an essay in MLA as opposed to APA format doesn't scream out queer politics either. But how students conduct analyses and produce documents are certainly gendered: Group work and collaboration are rife with gendered interaction, and writing processes and attitudes certainly reflect similar codes and social roles. To deny the role of experience or the impact of emotion makes gender transparent, yet institutional and disciplinary histories themselves are frequently stratified in terms of gender and sexual representation. In their wake, identity politics creeps back again and reasserts itself. If women and sexual minorities are historically excluded from some fields and migrate toward others, what must the impact be on their rhetorical and linguistic environments, of what's possible and permissible as opposed to what's just natural or conventional? What might it mean to erase presence of a central element of who we are, or to so naturalize the dominant that the marginal is rendered invisible?

At a recent IWCA national conference, I sat in on a session focused on exploring the ways in which diversity gets played out in writing centers. Once given our charge by the facilitators, small groups broke up to address scenarios from a variety of perspectives, ranging from policy and training to recruitment and management issues. My group focused on a scenario that dealt with an issue of sexuality. About five minutes into our discussion, the conversation took an odd direction. Participants asked what policies our writing centers have for staff members who are "flamboyantly" or "openly" gay. One person specifically asked, should tutors be allowed to wear t-shirts imprinted with an "I kissed a boy" slogan if they're men? Another person responded by saying her center's director has taken care of "that problem" with "the gays," by issuing a dress code where men were required to wear collared shirts and women blouses. What if, I wondered, instead of statement-making t-shirts, a woman just wanted to wear a nice oxford shirt, or some guy a loose, billowing shirt. As much as I was struck by the dilemmas and responses offered, I was also surprised that the conversation was happening at all. The talk developed like no one present was him/herself a member of a sexual minority. I glanced away, perplexed, trying to see if anyone would meet that gaze and affirm, via grimacing, rolling eyes, whatever, that I wasn't just experiencing the moment in my head, the product of an overactive, hypersensitive imagination.[16] Later I would learn that other queer people in the small group were just as struck, but couldn't speak up. I wound up raising my hand and awkwardly came out as one of "those people," a queer in their midst, present but not visible, inadvertently passing as one of the majority. Even later, when I was telling the story of that moment to a straight colleague, he too questioned why any director wouldn't stop a staff member from "flaunting" or making an issue of their sexuality. Further stunned, I moved on. The whole experience reminded me of the power of invisibility and the dominance of assimilation.

In his 2007 *Covering*, Kenji Yoshino speaks directly to the pressures and pitfalls that gender and sexuality assimilation place on individuals in public settings. Women, he argues, confront dual threats, presenting faces that can't be either too feminine or masculine. If they signify

---

16.   I thought, as a director, my first question would be, "How well are these tutors performing? Are they solid, effective mentors? Otherwise, what's all the fuss? Students and tutors ought to be allowed self-expression so long as it isn't offensive or overtly distracting in the immediate context.

in ways too gendered, they are not taken seriously enough, but if they signify in ways that step outside of norms, they're seen as threatening. We only need to look to contemporary politics and the plight Hillary Clinton faced as she ran for the Democratic nomination for President in 2008. She was suspect if viewed as too brash, calculating, or outspoken, yet she was branded as pandering if she displayed emotion or vulnerability or challenged the gendered way in which she had been treated. Gay people face a similar paradox, but only in specific contexts where their visibility has become safe. Sexual minorities who cover (or are covered), Yoshino argues, perform in gender normalized ways, participate in the dominant culture without upsetting its routines, don't insert their identity into interaction as a rhetorical gesture to persuade people, and can't advertise a cohesive, functional community beyond the mainstream. The experience at the writing center conference represented an occasion where my sexuality was passing so seamlessly that the straight people in the audience felt safe to speak in ways they'd likely never do otherwise. For a moment, I was one of *them*. I still wonder whether people would have spoken in the same way had we gays been more visible.

When I now return to the moment with Kyle that I shared at the beginning of the chapter, I wonder whether I've covered my identity, my face, with my tutors, made who I am palpable in ways I'd never do at home or in my community. If we were closer, if they knew more about me, my life, I wouldn't feel so covered. The student with whom Kyle works is just as vexing. He testifies to the smooth operation of heterosexuality and the naïve dogma that can accompany it in his assumption that any reader of his essay couldn't possibly be an object of it, that his world could be free of *them*, that *they* could be an abstract concept. In this student's blissful ignorance, there's honesty too; he doesn't veil his beliefs behind politically correct responses designed to offend no one. In what he writes, he lays out open, raw, and exposed thinking usually reserved for the privacy of one's own home and security of one's community. In sharing his thinking, the student holds the potential for genuine learning through challenge and dialogue. Yet Kyle didn't want to meet him on those terms, to accept views offensive to his own sensibilities and to his notion of common decorum, as starting points to mentor someone toward a better argument, even if the position, Kyle thought, was immoral. Still, I can imagine, having been in the spot myself as a tutor, of facing down a session where someone needed help developing or revising an essay predicated on homophobic rhetoric. The moment presents an ethical impasse: Our jobs are to mentor and collaboratively learn and the content of one's thought shouldn't factor into that context; yet common decency, learning climate, and workplace environment dictate safety, not just against physical violence, but also the harm that can result from verbal abuse. Would we require an African American tutor to mentor a white supremacist, or a Jew to help an anti-Semitic skinhead? Why would sexuality be any different? I suspect it's because the tolerance we hope for and the diversity we celebrate don't translate into a social and cultural consensus about sexual minorities.

These tensions also play out in the world of teaching and learning beyond the writing center. Strategies to contend with them are no easier either, because context confounds how we can respond. In spite of academic freedom, institutional realities can preclude frank discussions, and our courses or students might be inappropriate or not prepared for them, respectively. Over the years, I've become sensitive to the reality that students reach my classroom (anybody's classroom) not necessarily signing on to be proselytized in multiculturalism or primed to embrace my subject positions. Most of the time, being queer—or straight or a man—doesn't have a place in the conversations that are ongoing in any particular curriculum. Frequently enough, talk does turn to difference, in all the ways that this book addresses, and I'm under an obligation to complicate and make possible a whole range of understanding, not to let any particular ideology go unchecked or position take on a naturalized status. This duty comes from knowing that not all ways of signifying who we are are visible in our classrooms, and from being aware that students take on journeys of gender and sexual discovery at different times. How we frame and make possible information can have consequences, productive and harmful, right away or days, months, and even years down the road. Creating space for this gentle activism and discovery can also serve to change education. Faculty across the disciplines speak all the time about their frustrations with and hopes for engaging students in meaningful ways that help material come alive and be relevant. One valuable way to make learning resonate is to enable students to connect their own lives (and our own) to their subject matter and to foster the sorts of critical thinking and literacies that assume their perspectives aren't totalizing. To have students understand the moral and intellectual merit of our partial perspectives is one of the best and lasting gifts we can provide.

FOREGROUNDING AND QUEERING SEXUAL POLITICS
IN THE WRITING CENTER

In the prior section, I explored the dynamics by which gender and sexual identities don't just get normalized, but also foster accommodation to the exclusion of difference. I want to shift gears and return to notions of opposition and subversion in the context of these identity formations with an eye toward how every move (conscious or otherwise) to enforce or enact a "natural" or normative position, always presupposes a range of possible identities that aren't. Opposing heteronormativity in society today might seem common or routine. Beyond transitory moments with political correctness in mixed social situations, I find the sway of dominant assumptions around gender and sexuality as hegemonic as ever. From comedic asides on game shows ("Don't get me wrong, I didn't mean it *that* way," one guy says to another) to stock representations throughout popular culture (the desexualized gay friend, the "Don't ask, don't tell" talk show host or news anchor), gender and sexual norms are no less rigid, even if more nuanced today. In everyday life, I've seen colleagues invoke their marriages and families to duck out of extracurricular duty and to police my own relationships ("You'd understand if you had children." "Well, we're *actually* married, so..."). A journey down the bureaucratic path to register and use domestic partner benefits is so byzantine and daunting that it's really not worth the effort, yet were I to marry the first woman I met on the street, she'd immediately have access to my benefits. Friends keep legal powers of attorney and living wills with my partner and me, hoping if a medical crisis were to arise, we could serve as a third party who can attest and vouch for their relationships, particularly in places where hospitals have no compelling legal need to respect same-sex partners. Being oppositional—even separatist, in this context—in order to pull it off with security, is an understandable position for sexual minorities to take. In reaction to a society and mainstream culture that kills by a million cuts, many work to stave off this everyday oppression and create safe houses, spaces where no one fears physical or discursive violence. The world beyond can be destructive enough. Given this ongoing experience with what can feel like an onslaught against self and community, I appreciate the moments when "grrl power" comes to the rescue, and women turn inward and coalesce, intentionally excluding men, to develop networks of mutual support and response. In those moments, a community provides safety and shared history and experience, a bond ties people, providing profound existential, even spiritual, connections that render translation unnecessary.

When I think of oppositional folks in writing centers, I see consultants and colleagues who refuse to conform to dominant expectations of gender and sexuality, regardless of whether institutional culture is warm or cool to them. Most are not performing their opposition in a self-conscious manner; they perform their personages as a matter of course, not as street theater for public benefit. These folks are oppositional at their core, characters whose affects and personalities have long roots and authenticity even when they've been arguably cultivated to intensify their individuality. I see Larry, a former graduate student colleague of my partner, who comfortably navigated a persona that bobbed and weaved from queer or transgender to working class and anywhere in between (he proudly identified as "white trash"), coming to tutor as often as not in a Dress Barn moo-moo as in jeans and an over-sized sweatshirt. I picture Christina, a young lesbian who tutored for me, who I knew was gay even before she came out to me and her peers in a class. I knew how to read her, and she me. I saw her play out crushes and heartbreak, even though we never directly talked. Around the country, in and around writing centers, I think of colleagues whose sexuality precedes them, whether they identify as queer or not, as a political sexual minority or not. I'm most proud of friends like Michele, Kami, Jay, and John, who are role models and path-makers for sexual minorities, young or fully-grown alike. I wish I were as strong and confident as they are. They live out loud and proud, without apology or invisibility.

Juxtaposed to these folks who refuse to blend or to cover themselves, a whole other set of people have a performativity that also fundamentally challenges dominant codes of gender. It's not an issue of strategic refusal, rather one in which the way they signify plays upon cues that people wrongly construe. I often joke that these people throw off my radar (gay-dar) for reading and accurately interpreting gender and sexuality. For example, Sensitive-New-Age-Guys (SNAGs) whose emotive manners and affect constantly throw me off. I confuse these SNAGs as gay men because they display our stereotypes of comfort with women, speak into their feelings, and appear vulnerable. They are the Kurt Cobains of the world, soulful men quick to hug and secure with caring. He's the metrosexual or skateboarder dude who exists in stark contrast to the oafish fraternity or sports guy who one of my colleagues once witnessed sitting in class flexing his biceps for self-glorification or some imagined audience to marvel at. In my writing centers, I have a range of male tutors, frequently SNAGs, from the young Professor Kingfield-types to the granola guys, each intuitive, gentle, empathetic, and active listeners. Women, for their part, seem to have a wider range of femininity that makes reading their codes just as difficult. From the "sporty spice" athletic types to the earthy free spirits, their identities aren't often subject to such scrutiny and negotiation. These people who throw off my radar are powerful to me because they contest dominant codes, not by rejecting and setting up new possibilities for signifying, but by working, consciously or not, to get past identity, to make it so fluid and illusive that it's meaningless or refuses to let signifiers stick. For this generation of young people coming of age, a post-identity world just might be very well plausible in very liberal, tolerant communities. However, by and large, pressure to conform to relatively rigid norms of performativity is now the stuff of legends. Behind nearly every high school and college mass shooting is an ostracized individual, and the proliferation of anti-bullying policy and laws across the states and school districts signal wide-spread harassment of queer or queer-appearing youth.

To be visible, speak out, or perform gender and sexuality in oppositional ways is powerful and requires a self-assuredness and sense of safety that I don't myself possess. Confronting and challenging dominance in explicit ways represents confidence in one's own agency to make change or flout conventions. As I've mentioned in other chapters, action can't always be understood in such binary terms of assimilation and opposition. In some situations, the consequences of rejecting the hegemonic pose real material consequences: the loss of a job and earnings, the threat of violence, the possibility of isolation. Those spaces and conditions make the question of agency more complicated and nuanced. If a cloud of threat, actual or perceived, hangs over a decision to cover or not, regardless of the situation, then to what degree is choice genuine or done under duress? Although I'm "out" to anyone who inquires, I rarely foreground my identity in public situations. In most respects, I'm the covering gay man that Yoshino writes about, not because I harbor any deep-seated shame about who I am. It'd be easy for me to blame institutional or situational contexts, but I rarely encounter spaces that aren't safe or inclusive. Regardless, what might otherwise seem assimilationist represents moves toward subversion, a set of responses which cope with power relations in the everyday. For the majority of queer youth, especially for those who have come to terms with their identity, they are masters of Logue's (1981) rhetorical readiness and disguise and signifyin' that Gates (1986) speak into. As I've written about elsewhere, maintaining liminality as a central feature of pedagogy might be the best of what queering writing centers has to offer (Denny, 2005). This sort of borderland practice underscores a transitory, fluid existence that disrupts the polarity of margin and center, forcing one to bleed into the other. Even better, in writing centers, these contact zones champion discursive complication and the (de)mystification of process, rhetoric, and audience. A subversive, even queer, writing center practice turns on tutors and clients alike coming to recognize the arbitrary nature of the dominant, enabling both to make strategic decisions to play along or to create cogent responses should they choose to resist or further challenge and question. By making conferences potential spaces to challenge what's natural or not, conventional or not, received wisdom or not, our pedagogy makes possible and internalizes widely transferable critical thinking and active learning, both of which lead to stronger, more engaged staff and students, vibrant intellectual communities, and better citizenship, whether on campus or beyond.

Challenging the status quo or received wisdom is part and parcel of what happens on any campus. Such critical and active thinking doesn't just propel the life of writing centers; it's the stuff of dynamic learning and teaching across the disciplines in college life. The everyday practice of dialogue, of push and pull, of problem-posing, and of collaborative learning is rife with productive conflict and with transformative possibilities for coming to understand self, classrooms, communities, and society. How we come to naturalize and/or disrupt identities in writing centers, however these subject positions are understood, articulated, and performed, can't be confined to these spaces. Teaching and learning beyond them need to interrogate how forms of gender and sexuality are naturalized, promoted, marginalized, and elided, where appropriate. As often as not, disciplinary context will preclude such discussions. Where and when we ask students to make concepts and material relevant with their own experience, and when we choose relevant examples to scaffold to them, we can provide occasions to challenge, not reify what's hegemonic. In that questioning, possibility is born, to learn and grow and to become and explore. On occasion, a person with a marginalized identity gains confidence to persist in the face of prevailing winds that trumpet convention. For another, it's the courage to contest those conventions and chart a path of one's own. Our writing centers and classrooms will not always be the arenas where people "come out" to themselves or the public; still, consultants, directors, professors, and administrators must resolve themselves to the reality that it will happen and anticipate their role (and its ethics) in the negotiations of gender and sexual identities.

PARTING THOUGHTS

This chapter began with two scenarios, one with Kyle that I experienced and another relayed to me (but lived in another context). With Kyle, I'm not sure I had all the right answers, but I was fully aware of the modeling I was obliged to provide. The response had to create a space for the student and Kyle to not make assumptions about audience, whether rhetorical or interpersonal, and it had to anticipate Kyle's and his client's own journeys to self-identity as well as those for the sexual minorities very likely present but not known or named in their lives. As one of those sexual Others that both may or may not have been aware of in their lives, I felt the uncomfortable obligation to respond as spokesperson for my community and as a reasoned, rational faculty member. It meant checking the visceral and reacting in a calm, cool, and collected manner that today I can't help thinking signified in ways that made me seem far more amenable to everyday, naturalized homophobia. In a similar vein, with the student who insisted on treating women badly, he was never quite a boor, but never performed the gentile sensibility we presume (yet never speak of or through) in conferences and classrooms. There again, no response comes to mind that feels like it does justice to the gender and sexual violence that happens to women in symbolic and real ways *and* that ensures our ideals of meeting anyone on their own terms. I wonder today, when I witness routine sexism, when and how I must intervene. Failing to speak against or to even create the conditions to contest the inertia of everyday oppression or heteronormativity, in effect, leads to complicity on some level. I don't know that we can pick every occasion to battle, but I do believe we must consider using strategic moments, where appropriate, as productive occasions for learning, teaching, and, most import, social justice.

Returning to the notion of fluidity between margin and center that I've mentioned at the end of each chapter, it's not a question of one or the other, of swapping out positions. I just don't see a world where sexual minorities are no longer stigmatized or marginalized. So much of our society and culture and their structures and institutions are predicated on binary notions of gender and sexual identity; to disrupt the hegemonic would indeed be revolutionary change, utopian even. But it's like wishing away capitalism because it doesn't work so well for some, however large that population of some is. The rest benefit to such a degree that's there's no compelling reason to change, to brake the inertia behind it. When I think of the face of the writing center, when I look out across the floor at who is coming to the space and works there, I'm proud that we have a great mix of women and men. As I say elsewhere, that's just not always the case in other sites. But when I begin to dig deeper beyond people's surface sex identities that are more or less legible, gender and sexuality become much more fluid and hard to contend with. Like class, some people can convert or pass as the center; they chose to hide or render invisible marginal gender and sexuality formations. Conversely, the center or mainstream can be ignorant of the minority expressions all around them, making its dominance self-fulfilling and perpetuating.

When a student, tutor, or even an administrator in a writing center confronts the question of whether to be assimilationist, oppositional, or subversive, each position carries with it assumptions about power, historical context, and rhetorical need. Rather than demand of someone that they just select one position instead of moving between them, a more sustainable response might involve strategic decisions about when to do one rather than another. Unlike our race, ethnicity, or sex, identity formations and politics around gender, sexuality and class are, in the first instance, expressed through symbolic capital that each signify in relation to complex cultural protocol that are ripe for change, yet codified into extremely intransigent positions and meanings. While hope springs eternal that long-held prejudice and exclusion will dissipate like a mirage, the reality is that their ability to survive is well-honed and adaptable. Thankfully, so too is the opposition and quest for social justice.

INTERCHAPTER 4

Liliana Naydan, former peer tutor, doctoral student in English, Stony Brook University

As a woman, I've always found writing centers to be among the most positive and safest places to work, perhaps because primarily women have worked as my colleagues. However, because writing centers tend to be predominantly female spaces, and because women come to feel so comfortable in them, it's all the more unnerving when the safety of the writing center is violated in some way.

When I worked in an administrative position at one writing center, I encountered a situation in which a group of women tutors called on me to help them with a particularly pushy male writing center patron. At our writing center, we had a policy that patrons were only permitted to make one appointment per week, and this patron insisted that he should be eligible for a second appointment. This wasn't the first or last time a situation like this arose. Patrons often had questions about writing center policies, and tutors often had to explain them.

What distinguished this particular situation for me at the time (and what continues to distinguish it for me) is that only women were in the writing center— only women were attempting to address this male patron's aggressive behavior. The women tutors responded to the patron professionally (and wonderfully), in my view, by explaining why the policy existed: to help patrons of the writing center retain a sense of agency over their own compositions; to help them avoid relying "too much" on the writing center for help. (Indeed, this patron in particular had a reputation for relying "too much" on his tutors.)

The problem, however, is that the patron persisted, becoming increasingly angered by the tutors, and that's when the tutors—flustered, by this point— turned to me. Out of what I felt was necessity, I responded a bit more assertively than the tutors to the pushy patron. Instead of attempting to placate the patron, I was firm: I told him that we'd simply not be able to help him. My strategy worked. The patron left, and the tutors felt relieved that the situation was over. However, the situation sticks in my memory because I've never felt that I behaved in a way that came naturally to me. I felt like I had to play the part of the assertive administrator, a part that felt alien and perhaps somewhat "masculine" to me. In an ideal world, the kind of assertiveness I expressed wouldn't even be necessary, yet because the writing center is so often a predominantly female space, women working in writing centers will likely find themselves in similar situations, feeling that they need to behave in ways that don't feel comfortable to them in order to sustain the writing center as a safe and productive space.

Like so many of the other experiences shared here, sadly, this one too is common, and as Liliana references, the space of writing centers is gendered. What strikes me in that moment of recognizing the gender politics of our spaces is that we read and naturalize their femininity—that's what marked and rendered them visible—and we don't understand as signified the moments where masculinity is assumed, enforced, or dominating. I like that Liliana met this difficult student on his terms, but the situation leaves me wondering whether he learned or understood his performativity as problematic, even offensive, and what message, by implication, this student's behavior also sends to women (and men) who are the objects and witnesses of it. Liliana's response, as someone experienced and secure with self, was fully appropriate. Furthermore, I wonder whether we risk reifying that kind of behavior when we don't get at the conditions that make it possible, when we don't acknowledge, confront, and work through conflict when it's presented. How do we, in a classroom or tutoring session or at a reception desk, wade into a moment fraught with tension, but imbued with our socialized ways of responding (ways that are always gendered, raced, classed, etc.). As well as anyone else, I can attest to my own tendency to avoid conflict. Still, this is a conversation we must have, regardless of its difficulty and discomfort. Beyond the moment, this sort of situation begs consideration of the consequences when cultural assumptions conflict with one another: How do we ensure the safety of our staff while maintaining spaces that embrace a diversity of bodies, identities and practices?

* * *

Sophia Mavrogiannis, former writing consultant at Long Island University

I remember a conversation with a fellow tutor and friend where she explained how, regardless of where she is, her body gives her away—that it outs her because she fits the stereotypical appearance of a lesbian: non-feminine and tomboyish. In the writing center, she explained, this translates to a strange need to "compensate" for the judgments people might make of her based on her appearance. In other words, she worked twice as hard and to be the "best" tutor she could be so that students would, she hoped, overlook her appearance and her sexuality and just see a good tutor—as if being a tomboy or butch lesbian somehow discounted her intelligence, experience, and tutoring skills.

My experiences, however, have been entirely different because whereas my friend's body gives her away, my appearance conceals and protects me. On any given day on the street, in a classroom or in the writing center, I look white, feminine and hetero (not Greek, feminine, and gay). To this extent, I have the markers of privilege. This doesn't mean that I haven't experienced my share of insulting moments and mistreatments—typically in the form of catcalls, whistles, and odd solicitations from men— it just means that I somewhat just pass through my days fairly unnoticed and unscathed.

Disturbingly, I've come to suspect that students assume I'm intelligent and qualified because they perceive me as white, feminine, and hetero—or at least this is how they treat me. I say this because I don't recall a moment as a writing tutor when a student spoke to me inappropriately, asked to work with someone of a different gender or presumed sexuality, gazed or ogled at me/my body, made sexually insinuating comments or any such thing. Additionally, I look younger than I am, and I suspect students make inferences about my age that lead them to see me as a peer—an act which I believe helps them be more open, engaged, and active in our sessions, and keeps them wanting to come back.

Sophia speaks directly into the differential experiences of those who can't perform normalized or naturalized identities in the public domain of college teaching and learning. She attends to the ways in which all of us signify even before we utter words, not just the folks whose performances and bodies are always already read as different. Within the experience she shares, there's tremendous privilege and power in having the agency to pick and choose the terms by which she challenges gender and sexual norms and codes of expression. For those of us who cannot pass, there's a unique burden to experiencing the public domain that's akin to the inability of people to transcend their race, ethnicity, and class, to somehow signify without meaningful consequence. The obligation, then, isn't for them to take on the task of educating the world; rather, we—people like Sophia and me—have to pierce the centeredness from which our own privilege operates.

* * *

Andrew Rihn, peer consultant, Kent State University

Universities and their writing centers often focus on words like "diversity" and "inclusion." Like most buzzwords, these are easier said than done. This point was

driven home to me when I considered having our center designated a "safe zone"
for LGBT folk. The sign, with its inverted pink triangle, would let students know
the health and well-being of LGBT students was a concern of ours. But would it
possibly turn other students away from using our services? Furthermore, would all
our tutors be comfortable with the designation? "Safe zones" come with responsi-
bility, and some tutors might not be willing, or able, to go that extra mile. In cases
like this, when "diversity" and "inclusion" are on the table, who gets to be com-
fortable? (For the record, the "safe zone" idea never got off the ground.)

What I like about what's going on here is a complicating of how we understand
spaces and a refusal—whether or not Andrew's center was aware of it—to buy
into a concept purely for its political utility and the message that it sends. My
colleague Anne Ellen Geller pushed my thinking on the notion of "safe space" or
"safe harbors." If memory serves me well, it wasn't about writing centers; instead,
she was challenging the notion that any classroom or meeting space could be
truly safe, and she doubted whether we could (or should) ever even aspire to it.
The point that Anne was making, I now understand, was that no space could
ever be converted and made neutral, utopian, or free from the larger forces at
play in our society and culture. We have to, in other terms, figure out ways to
work with, and ideally through, difficulty when it presents itself in any context.
Even then, tutors and teachers alike don't enter conversations without interaction already primed for subtle control and steering. We have degrees of agency
to both create and frame conversations that people coming to us aren't necessarily ready to do themselves. We must act on our propensity for gentle, collaborative leadership. When I read Andrew's passage, my heart is with him, but my gut
also wants to create a space in writing centers inclusive of those who go against
the grain intellectually, culturally, politically, and socially. I want a space vibrant
with debate and dissent where queer-identified and allied students and staff can
push and pull ideas from a range of perspectives, beliefs and value systems. The
rub, of course, comes when individuals of any stripe operate from positions that
exclude another's right to be—theological, philosophical, and political positions
that are among the currents in the contemporary world. On those rare occasions,
how do we weigh secular and political relativism that is part and parcel of academic freedom against epistemologies of faith and belief? To what consequence,
once we decide a direction or course of events? What do we do when our ethics
of practice and inclusion reach an impasse? Suddenly, no matter how safe and
inclusive we want our spaces, they aren't so very.

5
FACING NATIONALITY IN THE WRITING CENTER

Scene 1: An older undergraduate who says she's from the Caribbean sits down for a conference. She wants to work on proofreading her draft because she's worried about her "broken English." As the student hands her paper to the tutor, she in turn resists taking it. The consultant then talks to her about the writing center's policy against editing and suggests they read the paper aloud together and to stop when the student has usage questions. As the student reads the paper aloud, the tutor hears errors with prepositions, verb forms, and idiomatic expressions. The student doesn't stop because they appear to sound "right" to her. The tutor knows these errors are wrong, but doesn't know why; she just knows they sound "wrong."

Each of the earlier chapters in this book examined forms of identity that are central to who we are, considered their histories and politics and connected them to the context of work in writing centers. A continuum that runs across these identity formations is their mutability, the degree to which identities can be reducible or made invisible to the majority. By and large, race and sex are legible faces, and most people don't seek to convert or hide them. Instead, those identity markers come to signify as collective identities around which powerful symbolic and cultural capital has risen. Class and sexuality also index central axes for community identity, yet their expressions, historically, possess different social and cultural viability and stigma. People of color and women don't face pressure to become white or men, for the most part; instead, they contend with social and cultural pressures, institutions, and structures that inevitably privilege dominant identities, forcing those on the margins to develop assimilationist or separatist strategies in relation to the center. Working-class people and sexual minorities face a different environment, one that takes as its goal forced movement from margin to center. Setting aside the pressure to become middle class or heterosexual, these identity formations also share with others the question of whether to pass, oppose or subvert the mainstream. In writing centers, the subjects of each of these chapters are quite common, even if the research on them is in its infancy. Just as frequent in our professional conversations, is the issue of how we contend with writers whose first language is not English. These people represent a struggle over identity that intersects with what is an ongoing challenge to American identity. For the woman in the scenario above, what motivates her desire to write without accented language, even though I suspect she takes pride in her spoken version? What does it mean for a tutor to refuse the sort of editing that she seeks? How might championing the student's right to her own language—telling her what's right for her—be just as problematic as policing authentic language acquisition? Is it possible for a tutor not to go far enough in a session, just like it might be a problem to go too far, to take over?

This book attempts to make historical, ongoing identity movements in the U.S. local to writing centers, their scholarship and practices. Race and sex have the longest organized and sustained struggle for equality with genealogies extending to the nation's colonial origins, while mobilization around class is a close third dovetailing with the country's ongoing historic transformations of political economy.[17] Each of these movements has had powerful moments of success—the end of slavery, women's suffrage, the rise of unions—but still has long roads to traverse for pay equity, living wages, and the end of systemic discrimination, among other agenda items. Sexual minorities have our own lengthy history with organizing, working for social justice and facing daunting setbacks. Composition teachers and professors in the disciplines often make students explore these identities as a means to foster self-awareness and agency as writers and to cultivate knowledge of the routines of social processes in everyday lives, fostering critical thinking and honing cognitive abilities. But as Omi and Winant (1986) point out, our national identity is a culmination and paradox of ethnicities melting into one another and producing a hybridity that confounds the mainstream: Our diversity exceeds any possibility for cohesiveness, yet our nation aspires for a common bond that's ever illusory. Our history and collective sense of self has a conflicted relationship with immigration, whether forced or voluntary, and other identities that claim citi-

---

17.   From the mid-nineteen century on, the United States economy moved from an agrarian, subsistence economy to industrialization and on toward a post-Fordism, where capital has become thoroughly global, producing transnational corporations whose products, jobs and loyalties transcend local needs and national borders or security (Jameson 1991).

zenship. We take great pride in professing metaphors that allude to our diversity (we are a quilt, a mosaic, a melting pot, etc.) and have folklore replete with rags-to-riches stories that confirm the American Dream and the power of meritocracy. At the same time, Americans have a deep reputation of antipathy toward immigrants or international visitors, often edging toward outright racist, ethnocentric and isolationist practices and policies (as the "blame the immigrants" mentality illustrated in the aftermath of the 9/11 terrorist attacks or recurrent economic crises and reactions to them).

Often those attitudes get projected onto language use, with tensions roiling over whether to impose English as an official language, despite its widespread linguistic dominance, albeit with a wide range of vernaculars each with their own politics and internal conflict. In the U.S., then, a specialized identity politics exists at the intersection of nationality and language use. As Paul Kei Matsuda charts, it overlaps with the 1970s democratization of higher education when non-native speakers of English joined other formerly excluded groups defined by class, race, and ethnicity (2006, 22). For this chapter, I take as its subject the role that second language writers play in the everyday work of writing centers. While our literature and professional conversations brim with talk of sharing recipes or prescriptions to attend to them, I've always been struck by the Othering, either explicit or lurking just under the surface. *They* are a problem that requires solving, an irritant and frustration that resists resolution. Of course, this quest for the quick fix or a magic pill isn't restricted to second language (L2) writers because the rhetoric of marginalization is remarkably common: What do we do with black English? How do we handle "under-prepared" students? Why do *they* have to flaunt it? Although so many of us practitioners endlessly lecture faculty and first language (L1) students alike about writing as a process that's individual, iterative, and recursive, we lapse in our deep thinking when Others represent challenges to our comfort with established routines. Instead of embracing what Beth Bouquet (2002) might call a pedagogy of improvisation, riffing off a client's needs and strengths, we recoil, anxious that we might fail, say something wrong, or coach someone in a problematic direction.

Just as often, we witness offensive comments scrawled on student papers or spoken in meetings, noxious sentiments whose public performance wouldn't be tolerated today in relation to other groups of people. Such slurs, I'm sure, continue unabated away from the "safe" contact zone of campus, but L2 writers often are the objects of public discourse not ordinarily fitting the polite decorum that passes for common talk in the academy. I remember a senior faculty member at one of my former institutions who would complain endlessly in faculty meetings about students in her basic writing courses, referring to the "Orientals" as "illiterate." Another faculty member would write in big red print at the top of L2 students' papers, "This is terrible!" or, "You're stupid!" and always punctuate his offended sensibility with, "Go to the writing center and fix your paper!" In both cases, I'm pretty sure both instructors viewed what they did as "tough love," pushing students toward assimilating into a culture, without regard to their connections to it or the individual histories they brought to gaining a L1 education with a L2 background. These examples are outrageous versions of more polite marginalization of L2 writers that goes on every day in writing centers, granted in more veiled and subtle expressions, but no less loaded with a charged set of assumptions. Tutors and faculty alike will often demurely say, "Well, you know, she's ESL." Just as frequently, colleagues who otherwise seem to have sophisticated understanding of L1 learning styles, needs, and practices, morph into figures who plead an inability to respond or attend to L2 learners. They ask, "Isn't there an ESL specialist that we can hand this student off to?" or "Doesn't this school have an intensive English language program?" While I honor the field of TESOL and the specialists whose research and techniques have much to teach writing center professionals, I remain committed to a mission where we don't offload work when we in writing centers and composition classrooms can equip ourselves to ask deep questions, conduct our surveys of literature, and develop local practices, just as we ask clients to collaborate with consultants in being active participants in their own learning.

When I return to the woman mentioned at the beginning of this chapter, the issue of accent seems the richest for conversation with both her and her tutor. For the woman, I'd want to explore her use of "broken English," a term that I'd find offensive if it were uttered by my staff, but a concept that I've heard people from any number of Caribbean countries use to describe their hybrid languages. Some have referred to them as patois or Creole combinations of French, Spanish, English, and remnants of African languages. For her, I suspect "broken" is a code for recognizing the linguistic difference between her language use and the privileged version for her classes and more broadly dominant society. Turning to my tutor's response, I understand her hesitance to take on surface error, especially when higher-order concerns or global errors that impact on meaning are wise priorities to address. However, the strategy leaves me wondering what problems lurk in trying to eliminate a writer's accent: What obligations do we have to educate students in the politics of their language use? Is it appropriate or fair to enable a student's false sense of correctness or ability, even with the best of intentions?

The dynamic lead me to remember two of the most powerful keynote speeches I've heard in my career. The first is a talk Paul Matsuda (2004) gave at a Northeast Writing Centers Association conference where he shared his own story about coming to learn English as a multilingual speaker and writer. Matsuda left the audience with a powerful message: He encouraged us to think deeply about our tolerance for accented language and what that means for our willingness to work to understand one another. Nancy Grimm (2006) has echoed this sentiment in a speech she gave at the University of Illinois's National Conference on Writing Centers as Public Space. Like Matsuda, she spoke to the spaces where people refuse to get past accents and the domains where listeners have an obligation to hear. Her point was elegant: Those moments of resistance speak less about the L2 interlocutor and more about our own identity politics and what it signifies about us. In effect, it signals a symbiotic performance, a performance to speak or write, and one to hear and read. Our refusals translate into silencing, a mechanism to shutdown individuals and communities and to marginalize them; our willingness to be open testifies to genuine dialogue, to hearing and making space for the Other at the center.

Each group must contend with face, but the stakes are differential. While Severino (2004, 2006), M. Harris (1994), and M. Harris and Silva (1993) have written about the significant differences between ESL and native-speaking writing center students, only Grimm (1999) and Bawarshi and Pelkowski (2003) have moved toward consideration of the intense politics at play in teaching and learning culturally laden rhetorical and linguistic conventions in conferences. Frequently, interaction is predicated on banking American English codes and practices, implying that they are static and non-responsive to negotiating use (and presumably that Americans are incapable of hearing accent or dialect). Canagarajah (2006a), Matsuda (2006) and others have fostered awareness of the need to embrace concepts of multiliteracy and cultural bumping as means to make way for transactional learning, but little of this debate has extended beyond TESOL or composition studies to writing centers. Rather, similar to their own historical positioning in institutions, writing centers have reacted to the presence of the ESL writers as "problems" to "fix." I want this chapter to push that discussion by addressing the identity politics at play when sessions address the needs of L2 consultants and students.

To better understand the deeper issues at play in the identity politics of nationality, particularly in the context of writing centers, this chapter next turns toward a common grounding in theoretical issues that circulate around the concept. It will argue that to know nationality is to appreciate the interplay of imagined communities (writ large as nations) and the discursive practices and consequences of citizenship. How people come to an American national identity as well as the socio-cultural ideology parroted through widely circulated discourses represent the tensions at the heart of a national history marked with tremendous jingoism, xenophobia, and a celebration of immigrant meritocratic drive and success. Just as race, class, gender, and sexuality are among the most powerful means of cleaving citizenry in the U.S., the use of language and how we signify is central to circulating, enforcing, and performing difference. Language itself in the U.S. is a common bond that unifies everyone (otherwise inclined to be divided against one another) against common protagonist, one whose dominant (or perceived dominant) language isn't an illusory common code of English around which Americans often rally to exclude. The object of this odd coalescing is the multilingual speaker and writer. From this foundation, the section then reviews critical insights from multilingual scholarship on important distinctions between experiences and language learning motivations of international students and permanent residents. The section closes by visiting the charge of critical multilinguals that teachers and tutors must critically examine the global function of English, the degree of tolerance for its regional dialects, and the pedagogical, socio-cultural, and psychological implications of teaching "standard" English to the exclusion of its dialects or other linguistic traditions.

THEORIZING NATIONALITY AND THE WRITING CENTER

Benedict Anderson (1991) says nationality has to be understood in relation to cultural practices that produce meanings, enabling citizens to imagine themselves as insiders, but just as important, to signify others as outsiders. That work takes place through a shared literacy and language that creates a common meaning and an assumed understanding. An imagined community, according to Anderson, is a national identity. It no longer is just a group of people within a common border; instead, an imagined community is a shared way of knowing, doing, and being, the participation in which (or the exclusion from which) has real consequences over whether the majority confers or refuses citizenship. Because the population of the U.S. has historically been in flux (ebbs and tides of immigration) the nexus of geography and culture have never been stable enough to serve as foundations for a national collective identity. On the other hand, we've never taken on the diasporatic identity around which communities in Africa, Asia and Europe have loosely organized. Citizens with histories greater than a couple generations (at significant distance from our immigrant, slave or colonized pasts) are much more likely to identify in terms of regions, states, even cities. As a result, myths and language work together as shared bonds for national identity. Patton and Caserio wrote in a special 2000 issue of *Cultural Studies* on citizenship that the American form of it has gotten confused about its role in national identity. It has gone off course, they believe, as a consequence of identity movements, the ones that this book explores, pressing social equality (or citizenship rights) for communities or classes of people (blacks, women, gays), without also simultaneously connecting expansion of equality with demands for social justice. Today then, we have achieved a wide sense of equality without any commonwealth to bind us together for mutual support. Nancy Fraser (1997), who they cite, believes that without attention to the unequal distribution of wealth and privilege, identity politics becomes rudderless and citizenship purposeless. In that vacuum, a competing version of citizenship exists, one with concern for the Other, This version has appeared frequently in our national history proffering citizenship by exclusion: a sense of collective identity predicated, in the first instance, on who we're *not*, and in the second instance, on a more expansive notion of who we'll *allow*. Patton and Casario suggest Americans have long-held contradictions for how we contend with immigrants who seek to become one of us, if even on a transitory basis. We celebrate the immigrant who embraces capitalism and meritocracy, yet we're contemptuous of the immigrant who fails or becomes critical, even suspicious, of our cultural myths (2000, 6). We embrace the success stories, and vilify the failures. We love the visitors who consume and spend money, but despise those who seem to poach finite resources to which our own citizens lack access.

Our paradoxical attitudes toward outsiders, toward Others, lurk at the heart of tensions over how we respond to people who don't speak or write in English, the enigmatic linguistic code that binds the majority together in this country. Our ambivalence veils our nationalism and unresolved politics and policy about how we perform and rally around it. But more than how English or which English or if English binds Americans together, the conflict we have over it is as much about policing our national identity as it is about performing jingoistic attitudes thinly tied to nativism and racial/ethnic bias. Ilona Leki writes, "Socio-political factors influence not only students' reasons for coming [to the U.S.] but also their attitudes and experiences once they arrive" (1992, 40). She notes that western European students are often warmly received, whereas African students confront the widespread racism that native-born African Americans experience in everyday life. Asian students, while embraced by institutions, Leki comments, face resentment from American students for their work habits and access to resources that their reputations warrant. Her insight here confirms the racially-tinged global attitudes of Americans. For students from historically colonized countries, we fall back on our national history of supremacy and conflict as those places struggle with economic development or represent levels of industrial and corporate modernization, innovation, and collective wealth that we now struggle to match, let alone maintain. Yet just as curious, Americans don't react to students from European countries with the same threat and jealousy reserved for other regions of the world. Europeans, as such, represent a nostalgia and romanticization over which Americans of European descent like to fawn, even if we're suspicious of what we project as their cosmopolitanism and moral relativism. L2 use of English—and Americans' tolerance of it—shifts depending on the subject and her or his perceived country of origin. More directly, face matters in this context. French or Italian-accented English signifies as urbane, while pan-Asian or –African accents are viewed as odious, annoying inflections that must be stamped out. My former colleague who derided "the Orientals" and their illiteracy had, oddly enough, infinite patience for continental tongues.

Conventional L2 scholarship makes highly qualified, but tremendously important distinctions between international and permanent-resident/immigrant L2 students. International students, Leki (1992) reports, come to the U.S. to further their education and expect (not always) to return to home countries once finished. The ones who stay typically come from less privileged economic backgrounds and families and eventually join the ranks of permanent residents, documented or not. International students bring with them, like permanent residents, wide-ranging cultural differences that make integrating with American students difficult, if not untenable. Some, Leki points out, view our culture as permissive and chaotic, and others see us as terribly provincial, with values and rituals entirely too restrictive and uptight. Joy Reid (2006) argues that international L2 writers are principally "eye" learners of language and are the products of language pedagogy that places a premium on rule-based grammar knowledge and reading in first and additional languages. She adds, "Usually. . . their listening and oral skills are hampered by lack of experience, nonnative English-speaking teachers, and the culture shock that comes from being immersed in a foreign culture, the language of which sounds like so much 'noise,' so different from their studied English language" (78). Typically, errors in writing reflect the cultural specificity of American English, from usage to idioms, as well as the interference or translation of students' L1 on their L2 writing contexts.

Permanent-resident L2 writers, students who come to the U.S. as economic or political refugees or as conventional immigrants, often have oral fluency in their L1 but have wide-ranging schooling in it that impacts on their ability to compose L1 discourse (Leki 1992, 77). Even when students struggle with writing, Leki notes, many have facility with spoken English (granted accented or done in cadences uncommon to native speakers), particularly when they are from countries where it is the language of commerce or an official language (43). Unlike international students, permanent residents seek to identify with or participate in American culture and resist tracking that separates them from their native-English speaking peers, even if away from classrooms or school they revert to their L1 environments. These "ear" language learners, Reid says, acquire English through proximity as well as trial and error (2006, 77). She adds that these students often have some level of secondary education, if not intensive ESL tutoring, that leads to greater cultural literacy, despite frequent L2 and L1 reading deficiencies that have a symbiotic relationship to writing problems. Permanent residents tend to display errors with grammar, vocabulary and idioms (cultural expressions as I would name them). It's notable that permanent-resident and international students don't produce radically different sorts of errors in their writing and that the focus is on surface (not invention or rhetorical) errors and differences. Further, leading linguistic writers also appear to suggest that the permanent-resident L2 writers share with class- and racially-marginalized students differential access to educational capital and resources that put a drag on their wider learning and achievement.

Reid makes a passing reference to the relationship between individual, community and society that is a powerful insight. Besides variance in family attitudes toward education and sorts of pedagogy students experience, Reid also points out students may reflect cultural difference that, "values reflective thought or cooperation above the analysis and competition valued in many U.S. classrooms" (2006, 80). What I like here is that she points out that even before we get to writing, before we get to its products, L2 students possess historical and cultural capital substantively different than our own. Our assumptions about how to perform in a classroom are culturally specific and reflect our eyes, our ways of imaging the classroom. It's another instance, as I mention in the chapter on race, where we can import and map onto our students terribly colonizing ideas about knowing. We risk implanting on students Americanist or Western sensibilities about teaching and learning, about the primacy of individual over communities, when just as often the epistemologies that they bring to bear have promised to transform our epistemologies, to enable us to reimagine the familiar through the eyes of another. I fear in our rush to monolingualist hegemony in our English classrooms or writing centers, we don't allow spaces to understand how the logic and everyday use of the language—of Englishes— by visitors, citizens, and immigrants, can create opportunities to expand possibilities for our own epistemology and expression, rather than coerce slavish adoption that lacks dialogue and problem-posing.

It's this unilateralism in our approach to English and mentoring/teaching it that I hear frustrating critics like Suresh Canagarajah (2006b) and Alastair Pennycook. Canagarajah advocates what he calls hybridity, an embrace of the dawning reality of multilingualism, understanding that no linguistic culture in these days of global media and consumption culture goes untouched by English, nor does English escape their influences on it, albeit more subtle (2006b, 216). He wouldn't assert that difference doesn't exist; what he pushes for is awareness of the implications of how it signifies and in what ways linguistic difference is used to reify privilege and marginalization, to, in effect, shore up center and margin. Canagarajah would oppose moves to any approach to L2 teaching where standard English is understood as a normative and students' own forms of expression were somehow pathological. He would instead support working from where students' own linguistic experiences rest, deeply understanding the choices they make in their literacy, and then pivoting that insight for use with other discourses and their rhetorical contexts. Pennycook (2007) shares that mindset and fosters awareness of the ascendency of what he terms "global Englishes," the inevitable geopolitical power of the English language, but also calls attentions to its potential for appropriation and resistance. As he writes:

> [Global Englishes] suggests that we need to move beyond arguments about homogeneity or heterogeneity, or imperialism and nation states, and instead focus on translocal and transcultural flows. English is a translocal language, a language of fluidity and fixity that moves across, while becoming embedded in, the materiality of localities and social relations. English is bound up with transcultural flows, a language of imagined communities and refashioning identities. (5-6)

Pennycook's use of cultural flows references what he understands as "cultural forms" moving between cultures and being used for local purposes to put voice to resistance (6). To him, the most powerful expression of that challenge is the wide-spread global appropriation of Hip Hop music and language as a cross-cultural genre of empowerment and protest, a form that itself is still seen in many quarters in the U.S. as subversive and threatening to dominant/mainstream culture (even as members of the dominant culture are among its chief consumers). In his use of "imagined communities," Pennycook brings this discussion full circle suggesting our language makes possible our collective identities. In fact, I'm not so sure we can imagine communities outside of the language over and through which we contest our identities.

Language, as this section has explored, makes possible our shared understanding of communities (even nationalities bound by linguistic traditions that transcend geographic boundaries), but it's also the means through which our practices cleave out who's included, left out, and the symbolic import of all that discursive haggling. In the next two sections, I take a closer look at how multilingual writers are pressured in writing centers and wider learning contexts to paper over their linguistic differences and to develop, practice, and perform in dominant codes of English expression. The drive to "fit-in" and write in a "standard" code of English that's constantly evolving and arbitrary is completely understandable. Multilingual writers face real material consequences for failing to gain facility with the dominant code—lowered grades, diminished access to graduate programs, barriers to employment. While understanding the importance and utility of accommodating the mainstream, I also advocate an awareness of resistant or subversive relationships to multilingual identity that writing center practitioners and others can offer to learners.

ERASING AND MUTING NATIONAL IDENTITIES IN THE WRITING CENTERS

The myth of the melting pot holds powerful sway in American culture. We imagine ourselves as a collective, yet the referents for what binds us are illusive, symbolic, and transitory. The protocol for becoming American or *Americanizing* oneself, then, is a moving target slipping just beyond reach, or a bar always rising (or falling). For permanent-resident or international multilingual writers, Kenji Yoshino's (2007) concepts of identity politics are especially germane. To convert their identities of origin would mean to surrender or become Americans, to somehow jettison what's intrinsic to their being. I don't know that that sort of change is possible since most multilingual writers possess identities tied to their race or ethnicity. American identity, by contrast, operates from an imagined community thoroughly symbolic and completely detached from a shared core ethnicity. As an amalgam or hybrid identity, native-born Americans are, ironically enough, in more of a position to attempt to convert who we are, than anyone trying to become one of us. Instead, multilingual writers face huge pressure to pass (maintaining a private acceptance of "original" identity, but rendering it invisible to the majority) or to cover (keeping remnants of "original" identity, but making performance of it non-threatening or acceptable to the majority). Permanent-resident and international students often seek to pass, wanting a public face that makes them generally indistinguishable from mainstream American college students. Eric Liu (1999) argues that marginalized people seek to overcompensate for their difference by out-performing the majority. The "model minority," he says, doesn't just try to be the ideal student through academic performance, the over-achiever; this student often tries to out-American American students. To cover, then, becomes a less intensive standpoint, one that moves multilingual writers away from the pressure to jettison the public performance of linguistic heritage but toward a negotiation of how they can perform their ethnic identities in ways that are acceptable to the majority. To replace passing with covering means no longer trying to erase all traces of linguistic capital and instead playing up one's acquisition and internalization of American cultural capital in language use.

Regardless of the cultural and linguistic capital that students possess, multilingual writers more often than not, especially in writing centers, seek to acquire language facility in ways that enable them to save face and to blend in with English-majority students. Despite the clichéd notion of the individualistic, carefree spirit of college students, conforming to received notions of group identity is a powerful motivator for multilingual writers seeking to write and speak like other English-speaking students. Carol Severino (2006) describes the assimilationist goal of L2 learning, the push to pass or cover, as "blend[ing] and melt[ing] into the desired discourse communities and avoid[ing] social stigma by controlling any features that in the eyes of audiences with power and influence might mark a writer as inadequately educated or lower class" (338). Severino complicates the pressure to "fit in" by noting that L2 writers must navigate the pull of American culture, its hegemonic allure for consumption, with the push to avoid stigma, to resist marginalization read through the cultural values attached to economic class in the U.S. Being *too* accented or *too* ethnic represents what my students from Asian countries problematically call "fresh off the boat," or FOB. When these students have expressed utter contempt for FOBs, I push them to complicate the loaded, offensive history of the concept. Typically, they roll their eyes and dismiss me, suggesting I just can't possibly understand the positions from which they speak.[18]

These first- and second-generation L2 students have sophisticated linguistic repertoires and are veterans of mapping and morphing their original identities onto American versions. They are quite different from international students who just don't have the same stakes or

---

18. Sexual minorities and African Americans have long histories of reclaiming and re-encoding formerly derisive terms or slurs. "Queer" serves as one of the more obvious examples of a term once hurled as an epithet that now enables the LGBT community to understand itself in more progressive, inclusive ways. For some in the community, the term is still fraught with tension, and its use outside of the community by heterosexuals, allies or not, remains complicated and unsettling.

motives to cover, even though they too seek to cover. Ilona Leki puts it best:

> Permanent-resident ESL students are likely to know all the icons of American teen culture but may be suffering from anomie, that is, confusion about which culture they actually belong to, that of their families or that of their new peers in the United States. International or visa students usually do not at all mind associating with other internationals and often feel more comfortable with these students than with Americans since other internationals are experiencing similar adjustments and problems. The internationals typically are not interested in being taken for Americans. (1992, 42)

While the international students often don't seek to pass as many permanent-resident students do, they share a common concern in many contexts of covering in the classroom, blending in and not sticking out because of their linguistic ability. They internalize and seek to perform language in ways that minimize their cultural difference because they understand quickly the price that students pay for not identifying with the majority monolingual culture. The consequences of stigma involve marginalization, diminished respect in the classroom by provincial native-born instructors and students, and inequitable assessment of scholarship and other performances. If, as Grimm (2006) and Matsuda (2004) suggest, Americans choose to have tin ears for linguistic diversity, if we allow accent to interfere with our willingness to hear and understand, then it's no surprise that students would seek to protect themselves, to guard against experiences that diminish their sense of security and place in sites where learning and teaching happen.

English is continually changing, evolving, and mutating for an infinite range of possible contexts (disciplinary, institutional, community, etc.), reflecting the cultural and social practices of a moment in time and signaling new ways of thinking, believing and doing. For immigrant and international L2 writers, this fluidity represents a moving target of rules and conventions that can't be anything but daunting. When I revisit the experience of the immigrant student that I mentioned at the beginning of this chapter, I see that she represents an endless stream of students who are seen in writing centers everywhere. Attempting to select the proper response to her writing makes me feel deeply conflicted because her desire to cover is understandable, a strategic response to a vexing moment. Without knowing her instructor, I wouldn't have been able to give her sound advice on whether her professor is the sort, like my former colleagues, who live for "gotcha" moments when they can pounce and humiliate an L2 writer for transgressing arbitrary rules of usage and style. Her professor could just as easily be one of those that Grimm and Matsuda would take pride in, colleagues whose assessment criteria have a wide range of elements that attend to task, argument, genre, organization or a multitude of other traits. For them, usage and style would still be critical components of a grade or feedback, but struggling with them wouldn't be deal breakers for an evaluation. While a student might not receive an outstanding grade, she could still pass or do well on the assignment for satisfying other elements that the instructor wants to address. I suspect students would find that to be a reasonable approach. In fact, Ferris (2003) has documented students' preferences for feedback that's both written out (narrative as opposed to symbols) and delivered through effective, dialogic conferencing. In the field though, tutors and students often are shooting in the dark when professors don't (or can't) clearly communicate their values, even rubrics, in assessment and evaluating writing. What's a tutor or student to do then?

An ethnical response to the situation, to me, is to process and name the dynamics and tensions at place and to work with students to understand what their professors' expectations are. From that common ground, we negotiate what's reasonably possible in our relatively short time together. Before we turn to their paper, we talk about their process and review the assignment, syllabi, or their memories of what their professors expect. Assuming we can't address argument, organization, or other higher-order concerns, I steer multilingual writers toward reducing global error that impacts on meaning rather than addressing more local error that just annoys L1 readers. This practice involves a read through of the paper together, where I note on the paper points I'd like for us to return to. It also provides an opportunity to improvise error analysis and triage what I'm hearing. To me, two critical moments come in this work: the first, presenting the constellation of errors and negotiating what to address first; and the second, helping a student understand that as they "finish" their paper, like any work of writing, it remains incomplete and in process. The improvised laundry list helps the student and me understand the scope of what we need to address, but it also signals that the student can make choices and have agency about what and how he chooses to deal with his writing. In their quest to cover or perform assimilation of linguistic practice, I want multilingual writers to have agency and a vocabulary for what they want, but importantly, for immigrant and international students alike, I advocate that they understand the arbitrary application of rules. More directly, I want students to understand, particularly in situations where idiomatic expression and other form usage are hanging them up, that rules are illusory. True facility, I argue with them, comes with cultural immersion, a process fraught with complications that must be acknowledged because they pose promise *and* loss.

To accommodate the mainstream as a multilingual writer is to acknowledge its sway and power. It's a strategic calculation about one's role in a society, particularly in the U.S. where the majority isn't often charitable or kind in its response to those perceived as outsiders. I'm drawn to revisiting the student with whom I started off this chapter. Her representation of her language as "broken" still makes me wince, but I hear that sort of characterization over and over again. It makes me empathetic to the motivation of students in this position; they want the codes and practices to blend in with the majority in ways that mitigate the stigma that would inevitably confront them. Anyone with the privilege and opportunity to work with learners under these sorts of pressures has a moral obligation to guide them toward knowledge and practices that empower them. We have a concurrent responsibility to raise awareness in the communities through which we and these writers circulate, of the power and possibility of imagining linguistic communities in more inclusive ways, ways that invite comfort with accent and dialogue about linguistic differences. Teachers and tutors also have a duty, as the next section will examine, to enable clients to make strategic decisions about multiliteracy. In other words, to understand the possibilities for opposing and subverting the dominant ways of English language learning and usage in the variety of contexts in which they encounter them.

FOREGROUNDING AND SUBVERTING NATIONAL IDENTITY IN THE WRITING CENTER

One of the great treasures of living and teaching in New York City is the opportunity to work with students who possess rich linguistic backgrounds. At each of the schools where I've taught, I have encountered students whose histories and literacy biographies stretched my ability to comprehend the complexity they bring to learning and teaching. One summer I worked with a Chinese national who slipped into an essay a cryptic line about coming to America locked in a container on an ocean-going ship. To this day, I can't pass the docks in south Brooklyn or Elizabeth, NJ, without thinking about what he had gone through in those weeks of escaping poverty in China for a life in New York City. Helping him learn proper syntax and idioms seemed silly in comparison to getting his story right. For his part, this student wasn't interested in dwelling or expanding on the experience. He was more focused on completing this core composition course so that he could direct more of his energies toward finance courses that were his passion. Then there was Sheku who was another client from a legal studies course. He struggled to critically think and organize his thoughts in relation to a very specialized legal genre of analytic papers. Sheku's spoken English was fine, but his written literacy required work to be at level with his peers. His ability to write was also confounded by his use of prosthetics that slowed his writing. Character by character was etched slowly, suggesting that his ability to manipulate the devices was still a work in progress. He never talked about how he lost his hands and forearms, but I learned from a colleague that he was the victim of torture in Liberia. Sheku had lived what I had only casually watched in the film *Blood Diamond*. Finally, there's Marina, one of my tutors from the Staten Island campus, who effortlessly switched from Russian to a Brooklyn working-class English and on to polished academic English. I don't know the story of her language acquisition, but I do know that she's one of my strongest tutors, even if too brutally honest in her assessments and a bit strident in her empiricism.

I share these brief glimpses because each student represents a movement away from assimilation into American linguistic conventions or passive consumption of academic modes of expression. None of these students seek to make themselves more acceptable to the mainstream, to blend in and not offend the sensibilities of the center. Instead, they seek to have a strategic relationship to academic and mainstream English, one that provides routes to material success, but that doesn't require them to lose their cultural heritage and sense of self. Being in New York City emerges as a powerful variable here; I wonder to what degree these strategies are viable because tolerance for linguistic diversity is relatively high here. Elsewhere in the country, where the population may be less accepting of non-academic English, or even their faces or differences, I wonder if these students would have the same level of confidence or sense of agency and purpose to move through higher education.

Juxtaposed to the multilingual writer who has a justifiable motive to assimilate mainstream American culture through communication practices, opposition and subversion are other possibilities. In all honesty, I haven't encountered students in writing centers who outright refused to perform dominant linguistic practice, so much as I have seen students who occupied very different worlds that had direct impact on their academic lives. Such students literally move between two (or more) linguistic traditions that take on a very autonomous feel. In this sense I'm thinking of the ostensible self-segregation that I see on campus that also gets played out in linguistic practices out in the city. I'm thinking of the students who only use English to survive in the classroom but then return to the other languages outside of it. I remember my partner telling me about a student who he worked with at his institution. She told him that her family didn't permit her to speak English at home, that there was essentially cultural separation away from school that was about maintaining and holding onto a cultural identity in the face of tremendous pressures to meld with the dominant culture. I got the sense that many first-generation immigrant families attached themselves to ethnic and cultural communities that continue to exist as self-contained units and that actively seek to maintain strong ties to their sites of origin. That people can maintain powerful cultural and speech communities beyond the linguistic majority—heck, independent of it—is amazing.

L2 scholars argue two anti-assimilationist positions under which these students' strategies might fall. One position, Carol Severino argues, is the separatist position focused on "preserv[ing] and celebrat[ing] linguistic diversity, not eradicate[ing] it" (2006, 339). By this approach, students refuse to cover or assimilate, maintaining agency in their own home language. In practical terms, being oppositional involves occasions where L2 students mesh languages where appropriate, incorporating L2 rhetorical flourishes and usage as a way to impact on writing and expression, to move L1 readers onto different grounds for understanding L2 expression. In a collaborative essay, leading L2 scholars discuss whether students ought to be invited to write in home languages, particularly when it teaches them to think and reflect upon audience, and suggest:

> Teachers who [invite students to occasionally write in a home language] are usually seeking to increase students' ownership and investment in

writing and also trying to give them a more palpable experience of a basic principle of rhetoric: audience and purpose determine genre *and* language choice. Such writing occasions might well propel students to go on and revise and copyedit in their home language. This activity will help them take more ownership of the copyediting process too. If a teacher doesn't know the home language or is not experienced in the home dialect, that teacher will be in the interesting and fruitful position of having less knowledge and authority about the language being used than the student has. (Bean et al. 2006, 229)

This approach resonates with what Canagarajah (2006a) and Pennycook (2007) advocate above. Not understanding language as either/or, but moving toward an environment where languages transform one another, creating the possibility for hybridity and L1 and L2 ways of knowing, speaking, writing, and doing to bump into one another in productive ways. I'm also committed to having L2 writers and speakers as tutors because they have much greater facility and experience to model code-switching (techniques of moving between and across languages).

Besides the separatist approach, Severino writes about the accommodationist L2 position. Accommodationists, Severino explains, are "not giving up home oral and written discourse patterns in order to assimilate but [are] instead acquiring *new* discourse patterns, thus enlarging their rhetorical repertoires for different occasions." Accommodationists advocate multilingualism as part of a more expansive embrace of linguistic diversity that resists the loss and colonialism associated with assimilation (2006, 340). In Marina and many of my multilingual students, I see the influence of this mindset. Marina's meshing of languages, rhetorical traditions, and linguistic difference makes her tremendously effective when she workshops papers. Problem-posing and challenging ways of argument seem like second nature to her, and the precision with which she coaches students toward revising prose represents an awareness of craft and structure that L1 students rarely possess or perform. Shuling, one of my tutors at another institution, would build rapport, negotiate focus, and conduct sessions with such amazing chemistry with L1 students, observers would often wonder if her clients were long-standing peers or friends. When she would conduct sessions in Mandarin with other Chinese students working on English papers, I wouldn't know what was going on, but the non-verbal cues they would give off signified just as well. For both of these women, their power and promise as students and tutors comes at the nexus of L1 and L2 and finding ways to work in the academy that haven't stifled one or the other, but enabled them to mesh and flourish.

PARTING THOUGHTS

I suspect that if we gave more space to multilingual learners to voice their preferences and frustrations, they would, more often than not, parallel the cues that we ought to take from tutors like Marina and Shuling. They would tell us of the everyday improvised use of academic and other Englishes; they'd likely share stories of collaborative learning beyond classrooms and writing centers; and they would tell us to both "get over" all of our angst about language learning and to "get a clue" about the pressure they face learning in a language whose codes are as daunting as the culture and society from which they arise. Multilingual writers seek to perform—to speak, to write, to be—like the often-mono-lingual majority because those sets of practices promise a modicum of safety and security from the discursive violence that they would surely face otherwise. Such damage is typically more psychic and amorphous, but nonetheless felt genuinely. The pain inflicted by insults can be just as injurious as real punches that can land on people. Still, on how many campuses around the country can a multilingual student—regardless of standing as international, undocumented citizen, or a permanent resi-dent—find true, unqualified safety? Recurrent media spectacles and political battles over national immigration policy reflect a wide-range of attitudes from outright xenophobia to ethnocentrism. And they are further complicated by anti-international sentiment both following the 9/11 terrorist attacks and during the ongoing economic upheaval in the new millennium. In this context, multilingual speakers represent a level of diversity seldom seen outside major urban centers, yet the wider U.S. political economy is not well-equipped today to cope with either the socio-cultural difference they represent or the ever-deepen-ing cultural, political, and economic globalization of transnational cap-italism that these speakers index. Further, since multilingual students will more often than not present bodies and cultural practices that sig-nify as different from the majority, they can often be doubly conspicu-ous. That reality leads me to wonder about their safety on campus and around the country and what we can do to further make campuses welcoming and to increase awareness of the opportunities L2 students have to share and the needs they bring.

How does all this connect to the writing center then? What obligation do tutors have to help a client blend in and assimilate or to resist and challenge, pushing wider society to adapt? I find myself going back to what Nancy Grimm advocates in *Good Intentions*: She suggests consultants imagine themselves as cultural informants, mentoring students, regardless of their face or what they seek, to bridge from where they are to where they wish to go. I remember working with many immigrant students who would preface their work with introductions that contained palpable shame about their "broken English," the same code the woman above used with one of my tutors, as if their language, on its face, wasn't legitimate. They sought to mitigate the consequences of their accents and literacies because they realized not doing so had consequences. One time, my client was a public school teacher in New York City, facing the loss of her job because she hadn't certified her literacy by a looming deadline. I never knew what kind of elementary teacher she was. All I knew was that she struggled to write without accent, the typical issues that the L2 scholars say are to be expected. Her essays reflected solid understanding of the readings that prompted the essay task, effective arguments and sound organization, but her prose was chock full of error—problems that never interfered with understanding, yet ones I'm sure examiners found odious. Over and over again, she'd get high scores in the general knowledge test and just fail the essay, thereby failing certification. After about four years of trying (and long since I'd stopped working with her and had moved on to another post) I got an excited email. She had finally passed. At once chagrined and gratified for her, I wondered, had she just finally overcome her accent, or had she finally stumbled onto a reader of her essay that thought holistically about the traits of effective writing and could read past any accent that she was still displaying? I wrote back to her and asked about her life. She was still teaching, loving the neighborhood school, and watching her own children grow and begin to think about colleges. The accent in her prose was still there, but I understood her perfectly. I wished my student the best and encouraged her to stay in touch. A flash of melancholy crept over me as I thought of my years working with those teachers, and yet I was embarrassed, wondering about the damage that had been done to her sense of voice, agency and confidence with expression by those classes I taught so pragmatically focused on test prep. I take solace that my work with these teachers, albeit immersed in the worst of current-traditional composition

INTERCHAPTER 5

Hadia Sheerazi, senior, writing consultant, St. John's University

If only I had a dollar for every single time someone has said to me, "You've only been here for three years? But you have no accent!" or "Your English is flawless for an international student!"

Initially, I remember being mildly amused by these comments made by people I met on campus, or even around New York City, and I would dismiss them with a smile or a casual shrug of my shoulders. As time went on, I began to realize that most people I met assumed that I was either a local, or an out-of-state student from the New England area. It was only when I would use the magical words "back home" would they ask and find out that I was not only an international student, but that I had been born and raised in Pakistan. The questions that inevitably followed were, "So did you learn to speak English when you came here?" (This ridiculous question has been posed to me over a dozen times, and, shockingly at times, by faculty members!) or, "You have no accent!" (I still don't know what this means). To this day, I'm not exactly sure what bothers me more: their complete surprise that a non-American can speak unaccented English fluently, or their ignorance (and audacity) to believe that I could only have learnt the language within the borders of this country.

Even more interestingly, I had a very strong British-English accent when I first arrived in New York City, and found it amusing that a lot of Americans were overtly impressed by how I pronounced my Ts. They "loved" the crispness of my speech, or even the way I said "herb". Unwittingly and perhaps even unconsciously, I decided to take on an experiment: I began to Americanize my British accent by replacing my Ts with Ds, dropping the "g" sound in the suffix "-ing" and speaking nasally. Within a fortnight (another word that they thought was so "cute" or "quaint") my friends and family noticed my new American accent, which was no longer "crisp" but was curiously bland as it lacked the distinctive tones and flavors that serve as markers of local and regional diversity (Brooklyn English vs. Queens English). The only times I tend to "lapse" into my British accent are when I'm public speaking (having been taught enunciation) or when I speak to my very "proper" parents on the phone; and every single time I am told by my American friends, "Wow, you sounded SO British just now…"

My ability to transmute my "English" to fit various moulds has benefitted me tremendously when it comes to writing for or speaking to specific audiences. It's almost as if I automatically switch mental gears when it comes to academic, reflective or creative writing or public speaking vs. formal presentations at conferences. I have no desire to "fit in" or "conform," if anything, I allow my nationality, heritage, multilingual background and perspectives to color my words. I learnt long ago that effective communicators employ metaphors or imagery that are universal and transcend regional, national, ethnic or religious boundaries, and I have never forgotten that lesson. Finally, the greatest advantage of being a multilingual speaker is that I have the ability to switch places with people, appreciate their perspectives and even condone those who are ignorant. I can't imagine life as a monolingual speaker, because I couldn't bear to just be able to see black and white, and miss out on the beauty of the polychromatic and polyphonic world that we live in.

I'm struck by Hadia's awareness of and insight about both the linguistic features of difference and the social-cultural response to her identity as an international student. Hadia clearly has the ability to not just index a "standard" English, but to move toward an understanding of multiple versions of English as codes, from the "standard," to a British form and on to a general American expression. Not many people are aware of these nuances or that even these can be further complicated by any of the identity communities I've explored in this text as well as regional versions. As we'll see below with Marina, that work with codes can move toward a sort of hybridity that brings language traditions together. Still I wonder, what spaces do we create and what practices do we cultivate that enable English with accent to be possible, doable in the way that allows understanding to proceed without the interference of accent?

From understanding Hadia's experiences here, I'm also curious about how her facility with language, with switching between codes and conventions or traditions, confers and represents a sort of privilege that she brings to communication that other students from her country or elsewhere might not possess. How do we explore with other international students or permanent residents the range of their linguistic abilities without being patronizing, reductive or essentialist? How do we resist the bias that comes from reading someone's body, affect, or language as Other? I pose these questions because Hadia's experiences are the exception rather than the rule in my history of working with multilingual writers in our New York City context, where the numbers of international and permanent-resident students are higher than other areas in the U.S.

* * *

Tiffany Chan, junior, writing consultant, St. John's University

Whenever I look at the schedule and notice a name that is spelt phonetically in English from another language (there's a word for it, but I can't think of it now), the first thing I wonder is, how much English do they know? It usually goes one of two ways, a complete mastery of the language, or stumbling over words with a thick accent. Once again, I'm weary, but this time because it might take a while for me to assess what kind of level they are on. If the student is Chinese, do they expect me to talk to them in our native language; do they expect to have a connection that they wouldn't have with an American; or will they write me off as an ABC, American Born Chinese, as if I have cut off all ties with my heritage?

So far, I haven't felt such pressures from the students. They don't expect much from me, only to make sure they're doing the assignment correctly or the grammar is perfect. Once in a while they ask if I am Chinese out of curiosity or if it seems I understood their stories personally. I'm lucky the St. John's University Writing Center and community isn't all about stereotypes for the most part, but rather the common experience that we have in class or on campus. The people that I work with know that we are all different, which is an advantage and nothing more.

Tiffany's response is really powerful. For consultants who lack her multilingual background, they can't even really have the mental conversation and negotiation that she is primed to do. I'm also drawn to the conflict Tiffany feels as a Chinese American encountering people with whom she shares some, but not all, cultural capital. It's that very liminality that this text has sought to address and highlight. But to dig into that background further, I wonder under what circumstances she'd actually work with a Chinese national or permanent resident in Mandarin, Cantonese or another dialect, assuming, of course, she has access to those languages. At a former institution of mine, one of my tutors often worked in Cantonese with Chinese students from across the disciplines. While I didn't understand the conversations, the body language and engagement looked wonderful, and the tutor reported rich experiences and progress. It has always made me wonder how writing centers and composition courses might make spaces for learning and expressing in other language and linguistic traditions, especially as opportunities to leverage for metacognitive awareness. I'm also drawn to what Tiffany says in passing about students having the expectation that after working with her that their assignments or papers are correct and grammar in perfect form. In the context of our values to appreciate difference and to make room for accent in language, how might those pressures from students be confounded by our practice? How do we address those tensions between our ideals and our realities in everyday sessions?

* * *

Marina Stal, graduate student in psychology, Columbia University; former writing consultant, St. John's University

As a Writing Counselor at the St. John's University Writing Center, I have worked with numerous students that consider English to be their second language. Realistically, there are students that clearly depict insufficient mastery of the language – is that a deficit?

It has been fifteen years since I have immigrated to the United States. Like my peers, I have finished elementary school, junior high school, high school and college within the American educational system. I finished all English and writing courses I've taken with no less than a B, but I am still labeled an immigrant. That English is my second language, although it is my preferred, is seen as a deficiency and a cause for uneasiness in regards to my ability to communicate appropriately.

"Do you think in Russian when you write?"

A simple enough inquiry into my thoughts regarding a paper I had written that inadvertently unearthed a personal desire to challenge misconceptions concerning bilingual immigrants and writing.

Being fluent in two languages gives me a unique opportunity to approach writing from two perspectives. This means that I can think about an idea I have in either language, read about the idea in either language, and ultimately write about the idea in either language. Yes, that means that more drafts and revisions are required due to the differences in grammar, structure, syntax, etc., but doesn't that increase the credibility of the final product?

I have worked with students that have told me their professors discourage a bilingual approach to writing and feel that it hinders them intellectually. I beg to disagree. Being bilingual allows for a more comprehensive gamut of the uses of language: English, primary language, slang picked up in English, slang picked up in the primary language, English-primary language mix, etc. The ability to clearly explain a thought should be celebrated; the ability to use multiple mediums to do so should be commended.

So yes, I think in Russian when I write. And in English. And in Russo-English. And also in Brooklyn-ese, St. John's-ese, Writing Center-ese, psychology-ese. I do not believe that a deficit in the English language is appropriate to consider a deficit; it is a learning process. Learning a language is learning a way to convey your thoughts, thoughts that cannot be created or considered without a desire to do so. If focusing on detail such as thinking and writing in a specific language, I feel that we are missing the bigger picture. Why are we writing? Why does it matter? Those are the questions that are important to ask, not whether a verb is in the proper tense. Tenses can be learned, ideas cannot.

What I like here is the whole set of values and politics that come along with multilingualism as well as the hybridity of language to which Marina alludes. She speaks into the stigma that multilingual learners experience in education and the ways that resident status confounds or exacerbates perceptions of cultural or social integration. If a person is signified as an immigrant, particularly from a different linguistic tradition than what dominates here in the U.S., Marina points out that that individual is cast as always already caught in that status of an outsider, a position from which escape is fraught with complications.

I also appreciate her thoughts about the presumption of deficiency that too often accompanies multilingual students: Coming from a different linguistic tradition is equated with an absence or paucity as opposed to a different range and set of experiences with the dominant language culture. At the heart of this mindset is a patronizing notion that limits the place and status of multilingual writers, and also fails to understand the intrinsic value a multilingual awareness brings to learning and teaching in this postmodern era.

Besides the tension Marina addresses so well, she also references the power of switching, meshing and blending codes in ways that make her language never pure, but thoroughly improvisational and multivocal. Coming to—even having—our ideas, whatever the code, is a recursive and iterative process that stops, starts, stumbles, spins, and spurts. How we come to those ideas, that process she references, is just as crucial. Still, getting to where we need to get to is important, but I also wonder how we factor into this line of thinking the cultural specificity of linguistic traditions. How do we embrace what's lost in translation, not as a barrier to dialogue and understanding, but as an opportunity to foster them?

6
FACING THE CENTER REDUX

*Scene 1:*Motivated by survival needs read through accountability measures and institutional programming, a writing center administrator finds himself mapping and charting, qualifying and quantifying all that he does in the name of delivery of instruction and mentoring. Under the mantra of "If you can measure it, you get it," the director hopes assessment work can capture and communicate the wide-ranging and effective tutoring in his writing center and that it pays off, in no particular order, with greater funding for the center, assurance of its survival, stable employment, a raise, and tenure.

This dilemma—contending with institutional pressures to measure the efficacy of writing center work and to insert accountability into expenditures of energy, time and money—represents a common experience in colleges and universities these days. It speaks into the influence of corporate-style management discourses and philosophy on college education as well as a historical distrust of and ambivalence toward education. Colleges and universities in the U.S. are celebrated for their innovation and excellence, but they're also assailed as a safe harbors for political correctness (from the left and right) and disengaged teaching. These clichés and myths have warranted wide-ranging assaults on colleges and universities: the tenure stream professoriate being replaced by contingent contract labor, students being funneled into overcrowded classrooms, and tuition being increased as state and federal support fails to keep in line with escalating costs. At tuition-driven institutions, pressure to please customers-cum-students and parents jockeys with academic freedom. Professors and administrators balance intellectual and institutional integrity with legitimate fears of dropping enrollments. Such checkbook education produces an uncomfortable paradox: To what extent can learning and teaching operate freely from the influence of not biting the hand that feeds? When taxpayers or their legislative and gubernatorial representatives are able to restrict and expand funding at the shift of political or economic winds, politicized curricula for dubious and genuine means are inevitable consequences.

The Academic Bill of Rights Movement, championed most prominently by David Horowitz, is only the most contemporary version, preceded by New Right radio broadcasters, and before them *Dartmouth Review* and impresarios mocking political correctness debates.

Writing centers and the professionals who work within them contend with the local manifestations of these larger socio-cultural forces. On campus, these tensions commingle with institutional histories and cultures as well as cross-currents within our larger discipline and across the curriculum. How we come to manage and deal with them—our everyday activism—provides critical lessons to our colleagues beyond the spaces of writing centers so long as we never position ourselves (or are positioned) as the site to offload, dump, or take on every difficult problem related to writing and learning. The scenario at the beginning of this chapter speaks into the self-understanding that writing center professionals and our units must interrogate, own, and shape. I've come to learn that my attempts to justify myself and the writing centers I've directed signify my own sense of self and place in the institution and profession. My labor to defend and prove also makes a statement about how institutions and disciplines make sense of those writing centers and me as a professional who directs them, an insight which isn't entirely comfortable or reassuring. Like all the other identities that this book has explored, claiming a writing center identity represents a whole set of negotiations that are never neutral or without consequence. My willingness to chase after proof of a writing center's efficacy casts doubt on my own ethos as a professional and the unit's status and reflects an institution's governing logic about administration and the expenditure of resources. In effect, I become complicit in an institutional positioning that's not fully academic, not totally administrative, and that brackets trust in my expertise for material and symbolic proof of it (greater retention rates, improved grades, more engaged students, etc.). Nowhere else in the academy is such managerial practice so seamlessly naturalized, so readily accepted. I don't know whether that's a productive development or a warning that the larger academe ought to take note of, but I do know that the whole dynamic positions writing centers and their directors quite differently. That reality has consequences for how writing centers are positioned and what status the professionals who run them assume.

Just as we've seen in the other chapters about identity politics, the question of face, center, and margin is critical to understanding writing center work. However, it's not enough to unpack how we do identity and to what effect in everyday sessions. We've seen that some faces are readily visible, subject to mainstream, dissident, and subversive understandings; others are coded to specific audiences. Those same lessons could extend to the profession. To continue advancing writing center scholarship and the intellectual labor of our units, we need a deep discussion of our positioning on campuses, in our departments, and in our wider profession. Are we on the margins or at the center? To what effect? Do we accommodate, resist, or subvert and for what purposes? Where are we vis-à-vis composition studies and English studies? Are we marginal or central sites for all that the field ponders and represents? What lessons do we teach about the realities of our work that can advance English studies and composition or rhetoric? What can we learn from greater disciplinary rigor? How do we move toward greater agency to traverse margin and center? How can we be strategic about the face we present and its impact? Rarely does a week go by that people don't post on WCenter or our local listservs seeking advice about how they can mobilize support for their writing centers, wishing to know how they can legitimate writing center practices, or wanting the collective wisdom of the community about how to improve a writing center's position in an institution. These queries are legitimate and genuine, but they also reference a certain paucity of standards for what it means to operate in this field that wouldn't wash anywhere else. As Michele Eodice (2009), a former president of the International Writing Centers Association, posed, would physics allow someone to pop up in a professional conversation and ask how to "do" being in the profession? Yet this sort of learning on the job is quite common in writing centers in spite of many arenas and outlets where people can receive professional training or education. What does that tell us about the state of our profession? Too often, we lack the intellectual curiosity or capacity to reflect on and understand what we do, why we do it, and under what contexts our moves work and don't work. Too often, we turn to the larger community and want quick and dirty recipes for what to do in a pinch. Instead, we need to acknowledge that beyond the received wisdom is a history and corpus of scholarship that needs to be engaged, riffed on and reinvigorated with our own lived experiments, observation, and critical interrogation. We need to, more directly, infuse our everyday practices with the currency of academic life: intellectual questioning and theorizing of what's possible. Otherwise, the profession continues on the margin, not by design, but as an effect.

The lived reality for writing center professionals everywhere is that our professional identities are tenuous and enigmatic. They reflect the constantly shifting ground of what it means to claim a career, particularly in a field so young and emergent that no consensus exists for how its identity ought to signify in collective terms. Disciplinarity and professionalism is slippery when people who claim a writing center identity come from a wide range of fields like education, English Studies, communication, TESOL, rhetoric and so on. What does it mean to claim a directorship as part of one's professional identity? Do we go to graduate school to *become* directors, or do we fall into this life (and fall out of it)? What might it mean, then, to be an accidental writing center director? Training can represent quantitative, qualitative, critical, interpretive and creative graduate work, while credentials may range from master's to terminal research and creative degrees. The Writing Centers Research Project reports that a majority of writing center directors have administration as one element of a wider portfolio that can include research, teaching, or oversight of other units.[19] In 2005, only twenty-six per cent of directors held tenure-track positions. A majority of writing center directors occupy non-tenurable faculty or full-time administrative lines, while forty-nine percent possess terminal degrees. Associate and assistant directorships have an even lower representation of full-time staffing (47%), with a sizeable population of graduate students doing double-duty as administrators (20%). This information again begs the question of margin and center. What does it tell us about the larger dynamics at play? What does it say about our status in the academy and to what effect?

Writing centers themselves, the units and spaces that are home to our collective work, must also come to terms with identity in their own way. The spaces take on a character and nature that are quite similar to any notion of identity that people can surely experience. I think of Beth Boquet's noisy writing center (2002) from which she improvises post-structuralist theory and makes a case for these spaces as liminal zones where institutional, educational, cultural and political tensions play out, never resolved. Then there are the writing centers as high tech incubators, spaces where instructional technology meets the hyper-speed of students' literacy demands and needs. How does a

---

19. The Writing Centers Research Project is currently located at the University of Arkansas. At press time, its website had not yet been released. It was formerly housed at the University of Louisville.

writing center signify when there's no center per se, when the writing center is defused to the margins? Other writing centers are monastic places, viewed in part as garrets where writing is produced in quiet and conferencing isn't dialogue so much as a shuffle of corrected and unmarked papers. Still another face is the writing center as clubhouse or community center. These are the sorts of writing centers where people can enter and everyone knows their name, students have rich relationships, and tutors know each other well and have a strong community. The problem with clubhouses is they foster cliques which lead to exclusionary practices and group-think.

In this chapter's opening scenario, the director is understandably caught in a world of reacting and legitimating. This person is caught up in what Anne Ellen Geller (2005) calls the fungible moments of writing center work, occasions where the tick tock of doing this, that, or the other thing elides any attention to the singularity of events. These epochal moments, as she terms them, make possible time for thinking deeply and for developing a vision of what has been and what is possible. Too often, I'm the director who gets carried away in reacting to the moment or lurching from one crisis and concern to another. I strive to be the director who revels in conversations that make me struggle and reach, and in thinking that forces me to believe and doubt. My failures and successes mount as the years go on. I remain committed to giving fewer answers and less advice and to fostering problem-posing and speculation whenever possible. To close this book, I return to the notion of identity politics, not to offer up transitory solutions, but to invite a sort of activist challenging of ourselves as professionals and writing centers themselves in relation to the themes that I've tugged at throughout.

TOWARD A WRITING CENTER IDENTITY POLITICS

At the beginning of this book, I wrote about identity politics signifying both a tactic and acting as a cover term for social movement organizing that has been going on since the 1960s. Identity politics are the ultimate postmodern expressions: slippery, irreverent, transitory figures. Attempting to pin down such movements to essences is tough, and their histories are rife with struggles to move beyond immutable and legible traits and begin to bump into their symbolic, cultural, and political implications. As I've questioned throughout this book, what does it mean to invoke a racial or ethnic identity in an American context?

How do we understand economic class position vis-à-vis writing and learning? What role does gender play? How do national identities and multilinguality complicate the teaching of a "standard" English? Writing centers themselves intersect with these notions of identity and the complications that come along with them. Identity is central to writing centers. and not just because they are institutional units occupied by the individuals within them—people with multiple identities that impact on everything they do. Writing centers take on the politics of identity and questions of face because how they present themselves has symbolic and material implications that represent a whole range of relations. Typically, people like to write about writing centers by invoking metaphors to better help people process them.

Andrea Lunsford (1991) famously posited writing centers as garrets, storehouses, and parlors. These metaphors index the doing and the action, not the collective persona that our centers come to take on, and not the identities that professionals that inhabit them come to possess. The writing center operates as a community whose identity intersects with the disciplines that inhabit it. Some, like composition and English, have greater profiles and influence than others. Patricia Bizzell (1992), borrowing from John Swales (1987), argues that discourse communities are social collectives loosely structured through and around a shared sense of language. Her definition helps bridge the "social turn" in composition, but creates a space to factor in our postmodern reality. That is, we don't have collective get-togethers and negotiate terms that determine codes and membership unilaterally. In other words, while writing centers and writing center professionals might constitute a discourse community that shares a language, a good deal of fluidity allows a great range of people to claim that identity or to identify with writing centers. But it's also that realization that makes things really complicated in writing centers: Ostensibly anyone can claim that identity; there's not litmus test or rite of entry. Put differently, because we don't have a code or widely agreed consensus about performativity, nearly anyone can claim our identity. A part of me wonders whether that's true in other fields, particularly in the humanities. When we move into the sciences, say biology or chemistry, a common language binds them more or less together, so that for example, when they sit in a conference room having professional conversations and what not, they may disagree philosophically and intellectually, but there's a common ground that seems to bind them. Even in the "softer" sciences, that connection might bind people too—psychologists have a shared code as do historians and art scholars.

Yet when we turn to English studies, the ability to share a common ground breaks down. Take, for example, my position in English at St. John's. I teach upper-level courses in writing and rhetoric through the department, and graduate pedagogy seminars in a variety of topics in composition studies. Though my actual philosophical and intellectual interests overlap with a number of colleagues, I rarely connect with them because my training isn't rooted in literature scholarship. When I collaborate with faculty from across the disciplines, they frequently approach me with sentence-level concerns foregrounded in their agenda. I've come to understand that as them reading me as an interlocutor and also as them narrowly understanding what's possible. They think, "Hey, all those English people think . . ." Then again, there's something about understanding ourselves as a discourse community, and I'm troubled that there's not really all that much of a community out there. What binds us? What is our discourse connection? As I look out from my office at the floor of our writing center, there is a discourse and there's a community that *does* come together. There's a way that the tutors talk, how they mark themselves, how they place themselves at a table or a couch. It's collaborative and dialogic, but sessions aren't all that make for a writing center identity. There's the moments in the pantry when conversations have the least focus on sessions or conferences. When the tutors are switching into a mode that is a hybrid of youth, college student, and worker. Nonetheless, it feels like a community, somewhere people can feel like they belong. Or not.

During a recent summer, our building on the Queens campus underwent a major renovation that forced the library staff to share our space and resources, a reallocation that went fine until the fall semester came around. Then the Writing Institute became a combined space of library users, the First-Year Writing Program, and the Writing Center, all working on top of one another. We became, for a couple months, a designated campus-wide "quiet" study space. That should have been our first warning: What does it mean to commingle a space already humming with conversation and activities, with a use of space, where people ostensibly seek out silence? Throughout the fall, people got into conflicts over whether they could sleep, eat, camp out all day long, or who could conference where, when, and how. There was a good amount of crankiness, but what impressed me most was how the tutors came together and made the best of a difficult situation. Instead of being spread out, the consultants often worked on top of one another and came to better know each other and riff off of what their colleagues did in sessions. Another unexpected outcome of sharing space was that we reached a whole new population of students who spent hours in the institute studying, a number of whom began to approach us for support with their writing in disciplines with which we didn't have frequent contact. My point in this story is simple. We face constant moments that we can greet as threats in our writing centers, occasions that we can interpret as assaults to our continued viability and sanctity. Or, we can choose to understand these occasions as opportunities to innovate and experiment.

In this sense, I want to turn to a final exploration that goes beyond the bodies that circulate through the writing center—beyond the typical faces of race, class, gender, sexuality, and nationality—and toward two other sets of faces that are present and have unique dynamics of their own. Writing centers as institutional units take on a face, a collective dimension with a shared morale and history that transcends the people who often have transitory existences within them. Writing center leadership and staff often turn over, reflecting the ongoing cycles and routines of academic life: people graduate, they advance or change professional trajectories, they retire. A mentor in the field once told me that a healthy writing center succeeds its directors, that an effective writing center persists regardless of its leadership because its process and foundations ought to be sound and self-sustaining in their own right. She argued that predicating a writing center on a single individual, or even a set of them, made it vulnerable to everyday events and dependent on people, whose own ever-shifting needs and demands would inevitably undermine a writing center's stability. This advice was powerful because it forced me to realize writing centers take on an existence larger than the individuals within them, that the face of a writing center isn't synonymous with its directors or leadership. The idea a writing center as an institutional unit co-exists in tension with another entity, one just as crucial and in need of interrogation: writing center professionals. These individuals, whether they're imagined as faculty, administrators, students, tenurable, promotable, or transitory, never neutrally signify within the institution or wider academe. Who comes to direct a writing center, how an institution positions them, and how these individuals position themselves (within the institution) reveal rich insight on everyone and everything involved. In a sense, these faces and their negotiations provide understanding of the ongoing dynamics of the profession and the building of a discipline that don't have analogs in other established academic fields. How we professionalize ourselves as well as the precedents we establish vis-à-vis other academic intellectual labor have lasting consequences.

PERFORMATIVITY AND THE WRITING CENTER

In chapter 2, I looked into the identity politics of race in writing centers. At the core of that discussion, of coming to know the role racial formation plays in the face of writing centers, is a dynamic centered on performativity, the means by which people enact their identities, racial or otherwise. People of color face a unique challenge in our culture since their bodies in action are always subject to scrutiny on multiple fronts and in ways that reinscribe their subordination in a society that is no less racist in spite of its own push/pull relationship to social progress. White people, who perform the racially-dominant identity formation, simply don't experience the same self-awareness (or collective knowledge) of the cultural and rhetorical implications of how they enact their identities as people of color do (LeCourt 2006, 34). To be sure, I perform my whiteness as seamlessly and hegemonically as my masculinity and American nationality command (I rarely question their naturalness, dominance, or privilege), yet my class and sexual identity operate as subject positions imbued with alterity that complicate the way I move through the world, winnowing the range of possibilities for doing so. In every instance, those components of identity or face impact on how I perform who I am—who I can be—because their material implications and rhetorical possibilities always weigh on my choices, as opposed to the implicit, instinctual effortlessness by which I enact the privilege I possess. Likewise, albeit with a profoundly different history, people of color must negotiate, consciously or not, explicitly or not, how they move their bodies through various racially-encoded spaces and to what effect as accommodationist, oppositional or subversive. That very nexus of race and performance—its attention to action, to doing in relation to audience, not just to being an entity—holds powerful consequences for imagining writing centers and the people who claim those spaces as central to their professional identities.

The Writing Center as a Performative Space

Organizations and institutions have existences and histories that exceed the individuals within them and their physical structures. These units are spaces that perform and are generative in their own right. In my Queens campus writing center, the space ebbs from a frenetic pace to the sleepy library feel that is its core; whereas the Staten Island branch has the vibe of being more cozy and conventional. Both spaces are outfitted with similar furniture, university branding of its coat of arms and quotations from historically significant writers and activists. In this self-conscious affiliation with the larger university identity and mission, these writing centers are fully accommodationist in their spatial performativity: they are positioned to blend in and flow smoothly with the larger Institute for Writing Studies; they are a face that the university venerates, from high profile spaces to strong, stable funding for them to have the greatest success and broadest reach possible. As a result, these writing centers are expected to demonstrate success in material terms, to serve as benchmarks of accountability, efficacy, and institutional collaboration that can be illusive elsewhere at St. John's. This sort of engagement and profile in the wider institution hasn't always been the case as Derek Owens (2008), former director of our writing center and current leader of our larger writing institute argues. The earlier writing center had a more oppositional ethos, a space that reflected its director's and staff's improvisational use of inherited space—comfy, rumpled couches, murals, and a lived-in feel. It was a clubhouse with a history where the tutors felt like they owned and put their own imprint on the space. Against this old writing center the current ones are measured. Not surprisingly, the Staten Island center, with its smaller operation and closer knit staff more closely approximates that old clubhouse without any self-awareness of doing so, while the Queens center chafes under its spotlight and pressure to accommodate its marquee status, romanticizing that smaller, older space all the while. My ideal writing center is one whose accommodationist profile is leveraged for subversive work. It serves as a space for social and institutional change that doesn't necessarily or directly benefit corporatist academic interests. At St. John's, our work building community writing centers and ones in under-served high schools advances that agenda, yet I turn to programs like Camp Completion, an intensive dissertation jump-start workshop at the University of Oklahoma, as an example of a service that transforms, empowers, and challenges institutional status quo. It becomes a writing center performance parlayed for making tangible difference.

Writing Center Professionals

Closely aligned to the performativity endemic to writing center spaces—how their positioning and action have material and rhetorical referents and consequences—the professionals who work within them present affects that richly signify. While nearly everyone in a writing center has a sort of transitory existence considering the relative permanence of the units, I'm writing here less about the undergraduate or graduate coaches or consultants, and more about the individuals whose professional identities have stakes in writing centers that aren't fleeting. As bodies moving through specific sites, writing center professionals present faces that can conform to institutionally conventional ways, that can systematically challenge them, and that can work to transform from within. However, I fear that writing center professionals too often don't understand themselves in relation to an emergent profession or that our community has yet to reach a critical tipping point of consensus for what it might mean to coalesce as a community, despite its wide-ranging institutional contexts. An accommodationist identity as a writing center professional might involve acting and presenting self in full acceptance of one's position in an institution. For tenure-track faculty, that might mean adhering to the unwritten protocol of weighting aptly and moving forward successfully on teaching, service, research, and even mission fronts, while administrators might encounter a different set of expectations to meet institutional needs (acting as participants in "service" labor, like committee work and institutional advancement bodies). Beyond the school, college or university, reconciling oneself to participate in professional community—attending conferences, dialoguing with colleagues around the country, advancing the profession—is an accommodationist move. Juxtaposed to it, one can oppose, self-consciously or not, by refusing to affiliate oneself to the wider discourse community of writing centers. I often refer to these sorts of professionals as those who "do time" in writing centers; they clock in and out, they may have marginal training and expertise in the field's scholarship, they may be effective, but just don't engage. Oppositional writing center professionals also can be figures who view themselves as contrarians within their institution, stalwart individuals who contest and push back or who passively resist the cyclical currents of everyday academic life. A subversive performativity as a writing center professional is more difficult to read and imagine; this figure acts on one level according to institutional rhetorical needs, yet she or he also moves toward a sort of everyday activism that demystifies the rituals and conventions of the academy. In this sense, writing center directors who act as mentors, guiding students, colleagues, staff (each of whom own wide-ranging needs, purposes, and motives) through education, possess a sort of leadership that's neither self-aggrandizing nor self-serving. This sort of performance imprints and leaves traces that pay forward.

CAPITAL AND THE FACE OF THE WRITING CENTER

Just as the racial and ethnic faces of writing centers hinge on their performances, Chapter 3's discussion of class revolves around the dynamics of capital, those practices that signify people's economic status. Action and rhetorical finesse shape how individuals, groups and audiences *do* and react to racial difference, but the very possibility to read that or any expression of performativity depends on learning, recognizing, and deploying capital. In the case of economic standing—class—capital is material (how much wealth one has access to) and symbolic (what it means to claim or possess a class-coded identity). The brilliance of Pierre Bourdieu (1984), the sociologist on whom I based this argument, is that the concept of capital isn't restricted to wealth, but extends to social, cultural, and political domains as well. Identities, in effect, emerge in coordination with communities that are defined by shared forms of capital as well as understanding of its use internally and beyond. To claim a working-class identity is about more than how much money one has, but also about a whole constellation of means of signifying or presenting face, particularly in relation to other working-class people and those viewed more broadly as privileged—the middle and upper classes. Ways of marking class identity include how people consume in every imaginable way and how we express ourselves through discourse and symbolic action. Words signify just as powerfully as people's movement through space. In the context of writing centers, class becomes visible—it rears its face—in sessions when students and consultants alike must own their marginality or privilege in relation to the discourses and rhetoric that dominate conventions of academic expression. In those moments of self-awareness of one's own position, those from working-class backgrounds discover that the language and persuasion of home, neighborhood, or community can be vastly different and seemingly incongruent. The academy beckons people to accommodate its sociolinguistic demands, forcing one to surrender the capital accrued for one sense of identity and agency in exchange for another—a set of codes that flow smoothly with middle-class sensibility. A Faustian bargain is struck where material security is exchanged for affiliation, yet to refuse it—to maintain or take pride in being working class—has real economic consequences (poverty, joblessness, etc.). Counterpoised to both positions, subverting both class assimilation and segregation involves a recognition of how capital operates not just for the privileged, but also for the marginal; in effect, the subversive face is an astute participant in multiple fields of capital, a traveler adept at morphing to the requirements of *any* community of practice.

Writing Center as Unit

Hierarchies exist throughout society, and typically they are associated with collections of people. However, institutions themselves have pecking orders, not just for the individuals that circulate through them (provosts, deans, chairs, full professors, associate professors, doctoral students, undergraduates), but also among their constituent units. Departments, programs, institutes, divisions, and even schools and colleges are never positioned in an egalitarian way vis-à-vis one another. These units operate in ways analogous to classes: they accumulate sheer amounts (history, institutional memory) and different kinds (political, cultural, economic) of capital that differentiate and reflect privilege in significant ways. Writing centers, players in this organization world, experience differential positioning in any number of ways that reflect their reputation and standing as well as institutional values and perspectives. Those that are sited in basements without windows clearly signify differently than those more visible or high-profile on other campuses. This sort of positioning dovetails with the history of the writing centers at Temple University and the University of Minnesota, institutions where the spaces reflect powerful shifts in the currency and sway of mentoring writers one-to-one. Writing centers housed as extensions of academic units and research initiatives exist on a plane separate from those fully identified with student support services. Who an institution staffs a writing center with and at what level, as I'll explore in greater depth below, indicates its positioning and ethos. For example, units with provisional professionals, inadequate resources, or infra-structure that's substandard or ill-considered speak volumes, even if the people who take up the material and improvise with it are able to make the best of a less-than-ideal situation (as many do). At St. John's, the original writing center operated along those lines for years, becoming a strong, scrappy center that reveled in its very marginality and could do much subversive work outside of the glare of widespread scrutiny. Today, that center and its companion on our Staten Island campus represent a culture shift. Units are now elements of a liberal arts and sciences college and a larger writing institute, meaning they are integrated into curricula in dynamic ways (the first-year experience, writing-across-the-curriculum, athletics, mission work) that the learning centers on campus just are not. What's more, because the institute is incorporated into the university strategic plan, support in nearly every possible material and ideological way is strong. But this level of support represents a local institutional culture that's responsive to creating conditions for academic success and following the lead of faculty, who in turn support the values that a culture of writing signifies. These writing centers also represent a long history: a movement to where they are now and a departure from another era, one much less progressive and innovative around writing and the teaching of it. For other campuses, the push and heft to privilege and support units like writing centers comes from other sectors more firmly identified with institutional administration, whose priorities and leadership can be exterior to faculty and academic units.

Writing Center Professionals

While the concept of an institutional unit accruing capital is abstract and difficult to grasp, the idea is far more tangible for the professionals who inhabit writing centers. Just as writing consultants gain competency and facility as they become immersed in the everyday activity of mentoring and the field's research on theory and methods, professionals also face a learning curve related to the same intellectual, social, political, and cultural capital. Becoming a professional requires consumption of the historical knowledge of the field, and coming to familiarity with an emergent "canon" relevant to one's institutional context (how, for example, operating a writing center in a high school differs from those at two-year colleges, four-year companions, or even research universities). Such collective intellectual capital in writing centers dovetails with wider knowledge in related fields and disciplines like composition/rhetoric, communication studies, organization and small group communication, literacy studies, TESOL research, linguistics, educational leadership and administration, assessment, and beyond.[20] Of course, it's impossible for one to have facility in every conceivable area, so another form of capital represents a person's sophistication with information-seeking behavior, one's ability to know what questions to ask, to whom, where, when, how and to what effect. Credentials jockey with life or cumulative experience for people. Graduate degrees confer and assume a different set of intellectual capital, particularly for higher education institutions, than undergraduate versions, and even advanced degrees signify differentially. Doctoral credentials trump master's work, and under certain contexts, doctoral types have different value and meaning. Even the institutions from which people get their educations represent an often unspoken hierarchy and privileging (Ivy League institutions over all others, elite/selective research institutions over comprehensive ones, private institutions over the publics, etc). Life experiences are also critical: Sheer breadth of experience factors into the capital that one can marshal. I'm a much different consultant and director today than I was when I started out in the early 1990s at Temple. I know more about people; feel more comfortable with silence, conflict, and diversity; and embrace occasions to improvise. But I also have more cumulative experience and knowledge than I could ever imagine back then. More important, my years of working in the academy enable me to understand its culture, structure and process; however, I continue to learn every day from the wisdom and greater maturity of my senior colleagues. This same learning process happens in the larger writing center community through its social networks (virtually through WCenter, real-time through conferences) and institutions (e.g., the IWCA Summer Institute for Writing Center Professionals, *Writing Center Journal*, *Writing Lab Newsletter*).

NORMALIZATION AND THE FACE OF THE WRITING CENTER

Gender and sexuality, the subjects of Chapter 4, further complicate the face of writing centers, and those dynamics are fully indebted to the practices of normalization. Like any other aspect of who we are, gender and sexuality are ubiquitous and require negotiation of privilege

---

20.   For more see Miller (2005) and North (1995).

and marginalization, dynamics fully embedded in what counts as normal (or not) in our spaces, culture, and society. The gendered or sexual faces we present may vary in relation to the different publics or audiences we address, and they enforce what is safe or not, what is allowed and prohibited. The convention around gender hectors all that is *not* to give meaning and understanding to what *is*. It presents a never-ending binary tango that imprints on every interaction. Similar to class, these aspects of our identity aren't always legible or conscious, yet for some of us, our sexual personae are inescapable and carry their own burdens. Writing center practitioners, then, contend with a terrain where learning and mentoring requires pushing students to work against the grain of what they have internalized as natural, hegemonic, and normal. Students must know that some academic writing signifies the personal and reflective as less conventional than the supposedly logical and dispassionate (and vice versa depending on the discipline or context). Interaction styles between consultants and clients can hinge on comfort with the performed or expected genders and sexualities, forcing both sets of individuals to decide whether and when to accommodate or resist the others' needs. In "queering" these dynamics, tutors and students come to know their audiences, reading them for cues of the plausible and fissures where subversion can slide through, not necessarily detectable to the majority. Such moments testify to transformative potential in the liminal space between the mutually constituting discourses and practices of normal and abnormal, a third space and possibility that's allied, loyal, or beholden to neither and both simultaneously.

Writing Center as Unit

Throughout the academy, the frequency and dominance of conversations about assessment are becoming legendary as institutions continue to corporatize their bureaucracies and processes. No college, department, or unit, especially those that want to maintain their internal stature or capital, is immune from the push to demonstrate the efficacy of their work or the value their service, programming, or curricula. Writing centers, as marginal or privileged units in institutions, must negotiate and formalize intellectual labor that they have always implicitly done: Writing centers are committed to problem-posing in the moment, riffing on the needs of their clients, and adapting resources, techniques, theory, and practice to the context. They make, as Brian Huot (2002) advocates, their everyday assessment practices local, organic, and valid (their questions and answers are congruent with one another). Yet the impulse to normalize seeps in and imprints itself in the compulsion to benchmark and standardize writing centers. In this accommodationist turn, a rhetoric of affinity underwrites the motive to shore up and rationalize local practices by gesturing to some fictive body of practices or precedents that grant ethos by proxy. Of course, good persuasive sense makes the politics of the normal wise practice. Quite often, appeals to the example of peer institutions and the ways they've supported their own campus writing centers (for information on everything from physical space to pay rates and staffing levels) have served me well, yet in almost each instance, my arguments were contested on the grounds of local needs and institutional history. In the metro area, the St. John's writing centers are now among the spaces that other institutions visit to benchmark outcomes (people ask, "How'd you get all this?"), and they leave mollified less by the products of my colleagues' historical labor than by the lessons that process, collaboration, leadership, and institutional change teach. Instead of abject resistance to the impulse to normalize and to document and theorize the range of possibilities, I'm intrigued by what these processes tell us about us and our institutions, and how they might be manipulated to advance and support a writing center that could otherwise be problematic. If a certification process engages a staff in a range of scholarship and literature that complicates and forces deep discussion of writing, language, learning, expression and beyond, what lingering harm can come from such conversations? Still, it's instructive to think about the disciplines and services that naturalize normalization and those that don't and how each are positions vis-à-vis one another on different campuses.

Writing Center Professionals

I write from what feels like the most conflicted of positions as a writing center professional. Unlike many in the field, I am an accidental participant in the sense that I didn't go into undergraduate education or graduate school with the expressed intent to work and build a writing center professional identity. Even more problematic in some ways, my formal training is outside of English Studies. As a social and cultural critic educated in rhetoric and communication, I come to our field as someone trained in mixed methods research, a combination of empirical and naturalistic inquiry, of social science and humanities values. Friends and colleagues alike often scoff, "He's really a sociologist," or "He sounds like a political scientist." Ironically, I remember professors and peers in graduate school saying, "He seems more like English person," or "He's just too much into theory." But when Frank Sullivan at Temple turned me toward writing centers and when my disciplinary mentors encouraged the move, I recall that they all had a commitment to what it meant to claim any professional identity, even if it meant moving afield of one's academic training. In a sense, they provided with me a set of professional standards for what it meant to be a participant in the field, to become an engaged director. Early on in my career that meant learning the research in the field—the key questions, debates, figures, the history, pouring through *Writing Lab Newsletter* and *Writing Center Journal* and then moving on into the books (Meyers & Smith's 1987 *The Practical Tutor*, Muriel Harris's 1986 *Teaching One-to-One*, Shaughnessy's 1977 *Errors & Expectations*, Bruffee's 1993 *Collaborative Learning*, and Elbow and Belanoff's 2003 *A Community of Writers*) all of which I wedded to my world of theory and criticism. As I've gone on, I've also learned that being a professional in our field means more than consuming other people's research, but also doing it (not just the sort that helps me move toward tenure) by learning about the local institution, its culture, and the questions and theory-building that they beg for. Most crucial of all, it means tapping into a network of peers and mentors of one's own on a local, regional and national basis, and then paying that standard of practice forward to new people in the profession, whether they are graduate students or colleagues.

CITIZENSHIP AND THE FACE OF THE WRITING CENTER

For multilingual writers, coming to a writing center is very much about how performance, capital and normalization impact on negotiating citizenship. In the academic life of American colleges and universities, acting and signifying as a member of any number of its diffuse discourse communities enables the people that circulate through them to feel greater comfort, security and place. From the social life of campus to its academic units, college pulses with odd currents of the eccentric, the esoteric, the conventional, and the innovative. In this climate, people negotiate (or refuse) place or belonging, by being embraced or excluded. It is, as Patton and Carsario (2000) and Fraser (1997), and others theorize, a dynamic where citizenship hinges on a grand game of binaries, of collective identity predicated on who a population allows and shuts out through its shared and symbolic practices. Multilingual learners, writers, and speakers intersect this contested terrain because education in the U.S. is inexorably tied up with a conflicted history of citizenship and nationality. America struggles with its immigrant past, present, and future. It becomes material in "native" resentment toward ethnic enclaves who seem to refuse assimilation, whether through language or social proximity, as permanent-resident immigrants or international visitors cling to common cultures of "home" that bind and eventually, ironically, enrich the fabric and flavor of the adopted nation. How one becomes "American," what that identity signifies, for whom, and under what circumstances is rife with identity politics grounded in the nation coming to terms with its own face and the very possibility of reconciling its inevitable diversity (not just a reality, but a goal, a raison d'être). As unsettled as this notion is for the nation, on its campuses, the intersection of citizenship and nationalism imprints itself on tolerance for linguistic diversity and students' rights to express themselves beyond the relatively narrow bands of academic English. Multilingual students, in other words, must struggle with presenting a face that conforms to the monolingual bias and privilege of the American academy, one that compartmentalizes linguistic use and citizenship (identities that are posited as separate and more or less equal), or one that seeks to transform the common calculus of academic citizenship through advocacy of shared embrace of multilingualism. I advocate writing centers align themselves with the latter position (as Grimm (1999) and Pennycook (2007) articulate in their individual works), fostering climates and spaces where transactional learning around linguistic traditions happens and creating opportunities for cross-cultural awareness that promises mutual benefit for consultants and students alike.

Writing Center as Unit

Citizenship understood as a community of shared identity and practices—a common face—feels especially apt in the context of writing centers, but I'd like to understand them as possessing citizenship in two, intertwined contexts: within institutions and beyond. Internally, writing centers are units that are parts of larger collectives of organizational interests. As I've mentioned before, writing centers don't exist in vacuums; they are parts of institutions with rich histories and often dense protocols that must be understood in order for writing centers to grow or adapt to an ever-shifting terrain. Geller et al. (2007), the writers of *The Everyday Writing Center*, turn to Etienne Wenger's concept of "communities of practice" to speak into the multiple and "shared repertoire[s]" that people daily encounter (Wenger 1998, 6). At local institutions, then, writing centers operate in an environment where the unit is part of a community for which there are normalized practices that require certain amounts and kinds of capital and performativity. For example, at St. John's, the institutional repertoire is punctuated with frequent references to academic excellence, student engagement and social justice. These values intersect with the university's Vincentian mission of advocacy of material change, empathy and support for those marginalized in society. Effective units in the university internalize those values and imbue their practices with them, and the writing centers have shored up their status by doing our everyday academic work through student-centered pedagogy and by actively fostering outreach and mission work that benefits the surrounding area (collaborating with local community centers and helping underserved high schools develop locally-grown writing centers). Beyond striving to be good citizens in the university community, I'm also drawn to the importance writing centers have as citizen-units more broadly, how individual writing centers can model for others a shared practice of innovation and problem-posing. There's something to be said for a writing center where dissent and debate, challenge and criticism can be harnessed and turned toward interactive improvement of the unit. To me, the most cogent example of this sort of subversive face to the writing center is the loud, chaotic space that Beth Boquet describes so well in her 2002 *Noise from the Writing Center*.

Writing Center Professionals

Taking inspiration from Paula Gillespie, Brad Hughes, and Harvey Kail's (2007) ongoing work through their writing center alumni project, my associate directors and I have started conducting digital video exit interviews with our graduating students. Cameron, one of the tutors featured in an interchapter, gave me one of the most powerful sets of sound bites that I plan on using in a montage of advice from former consultants to new ones joining our staff. He counseled his peers to resist judgment and to never be tempted to think they are smarter than someone else. In that sentiment, I heard Cam suggesting that future consultants treat every moment and person with fresh and empathetic eyes and embrace learning as ever-possible and rewarding.

I can't imagine a better professional sentiment or a stronger set of values around which to build a community. He makes me proud in that moment and challenges me to be a better director and leader by performing those values. Professionals in writing centers are part of one of the more cohesive and collegial communities in education. The collective embraces recent converts or discoverers of the field and its possibilities, even if the community itself struggles for consensus about its own direction and future. To be a citizen in the writing center field involves a shared set of intellectual capital and labor as well as a common concern for learning, teaching and mentoring. Because we practice such a broadly inclusive citizenship, it's difficult to pause and consider who and what gets elided in the field and the difficult conversations we must have to move forward or to complicate our repertoire. We professionals in writing centers intensely identify as a community, even a community of practice, but like the national struggle the U.S. faces, we aren't equipped to consider how our citizenship, in spite of its rich promise, is still deeply flawed and in need of interrogation. How do we come to think about who we allow or prohibit? How do we shunt aside specific practices and people and to what impact or effect? This book hopes to spur those discussions, but the possibilities extend beyond the forms of identity on which it has mainly focused. Our citizenship is never fully egalitarian or equitable; our promise lies with questioning why and advocating for something better.

CLOSING THOUGHTS

This book came to closure in the context of Barack Obama being elected and assuming the presidency of the United States. On the night he won, the moment was rich and powerful: Americans of all stripes cried with pride at the promise of what had come to be and what might come to pass as Obama took the stage with his running mate, their families and friends. Broadcast coverage panned enormous crowds in Chicago's Grant Park or cut to New York's Harlem or Times Square, and the monumentality of the experience was palpable. Yet in that moment, I heard over and over and over again commentators heralding a new era, one which they proposed was post-identity, post-race. It was, quite possibly, the worst possible implication to take from Obama's election, yet entirely expected in a society where threshold moments often can be taken as tantamount to social change. I know many voted for that shift, regardless of the party identity of the candidate, and I also know that that it's too early to tell whether ground has really moved or not in this country. I'm too young to remember the giddy optimism that liberals possessed with Kennedy's election or that conservatives heralded with Reagan's presidency, but today, I'm old enough to be deeply cynical about politics and politicians. In the moments and hours and weeks following Obama's victory, "liberal" California joined scores of other states in banning civil recognition of same-sex relationships, Arkansas outlawed adoption for sexual minorities, and Colorado banned affirmative action. As activists mobilized throughout the nation, outraged and shocked at the election results, I wondered to myself whether anyone could be really surprised that a minority, a barely-tolerated, widely-stigmatized one, would lose a popularity vote with the majority. It had happened over and over and over again, beginning in Oregon and extending to Colorado and beyond, a sure-fire wedge issue to draw social and religious conservatives to polls in swing states and districts. Against that backdrop, in Long Island's outer suburbs and in a working-class Brooklyn neighborhood, men were beaten to death for appearing to be different (as immigrants, as Latinos, as gay men). Throughout the nation, its greatest financial crisis since the Great Depression is sinking in, leaving millions without jobs and places to live, exacerbated by a credit scandal that played on people's dreams of home ownership. At the core of all this hope and fear: race, class, gender, nationality. Like the air we breathe, their dynamics, their politics, their identities circle around and through us.

To close each chapter, I offered what I called "Parting thoughts," meant not to wrap up discussion, but to provide occasions to spur further thought that might carry conversation forward. In this book, I advocate, quite literally, facing the center and attending to the margins, looking to our writing centers and their practices and becoming aware of the ways assimilation, opposition, and subversion come about in them. The faces of our writing centers, how they are marked or not, how are they visible or not, signify the degree to which the local takes up diversity, not just as a slogan, but as a central axis for critical thinking, student engagement, and teaching and learning. I've operated on the assumption that writing centers, even if they have relatively homogenous student populations and staff, don't step outside of the moral and ethical need to take up difficult conversations about identity politics and their practices to police, maintain, and make sense of difference. Our writing centers aren't islands unto themselves, isolated from the broader currents pulsing through our institutions, communities, and nation. They are very much local sites where macro-dynamics, structures, and systems become tangible and real. It might be nice, though utopian and naïve, to hope that the outside can't or will not intrude into our spaces. I don't think that mindset is realistic; instead, I suspect the harsh reality of the everyday is already present in our writing centers, regardless of whether we choose to recognize or go forth into it, develop opportunities to engage, and ways to process and unpack the commonplace of identity politics. The scenarios that lead the chapters have real referents with actual moments in the writing centers that I have helped lead over the years. When I've shared these experiences, they usually have been a part of a conference workshop that focuses on getting participants to think more deeply about how difference plays out in the context of writing centers. Just as often as not, people will ask me, "Are these made up?" "Are they real?" Once in a while, people will sigh, frowning as they say they've got precious little time for staff development, and with that dismissal, they will say they'd rather focus on nuts and bolts of ensuring sound conferencing is happening. In effect, these people are saying that their writing center doesn't have time or opportunity to think deeply about diversity, that it's exterior to the fundamentals, just not a priority, or merely an exercise in performing and enforcing political correctness.

I understand and appreciate that sentiment and offer this book not as a counter-weight, but as part of a comprehensive curriculum that leads to dialogue where the rich labor of learning and teaching happens. My colleague Anne Ellen Geller and I collaborate quite often and I learn more from our talks and challenging one another than I ever actually share with her. Most recently, we've pushed one another over approaches to teaching content in our graduate course curricula. We were torn between surveying a broad spectrum of content or focusing on key authors who produce sustained work with critical concepts. For the survey, students learn a menu of possibilities yet lack heft and substance, and the critical works approach provides depth and insight but can miss the wider conversations. Neither of us won the other over, and both of our classes had sound learning experiences and provided entrée into the fields of English and composition studies. More importantly, I learned, as I watched our students cycle through each of our classes, that they were picking up our professional values. They learned to cultivate colleagues, to listen and hear, to believe and doubt; they discovered the power of framing, its arbitrary nature, and its practiced implications; and they pursued research as a conversation with fits and starts, recursive moments and leaps forward. Anne and I hadn't (and likely won't ever) discover the right answer to how we teach graduate courses flawlessly, yet we modeled through everyday practice the modes of inquiry and collegiality that many of our students took up. That gesture, following our example, especially when we weren't doing so self-consciously, is the greatest compliment that they could offer us, because to imitate our collegiality, in fostering community in the ways they are pursuing, makes the pedagogy and change we value both organic and sustainable. For writing centers, it's not the prescriptions for making this or that session effective that matter; rather, it's the processes we make possible, the conversations we reward and make time for, the faces that come to the center, margins that change the center. To them, we're indebted. For them, the writing center exists.

REFERENCES

Alcoff, Linda Martín. 2006. *Visible identities: Race, gender, and the self.* New York: Oxford University Press.

Alexander, Jonathan. 2008. *Literacy, sexuality, pedagogy: Theory and practice for composition studies* Logan, UT: Utah State University Press.

Althusser, Louis. 1971. Ideology and ideological state apparatuses. In *Lenin and philosophy and other essays,* New York: Monthly Review Press

Anderson, Benedict. 1991. *Imagined communities: Reflections on the origin and spread of nationalism.* New York: Verso.

Anyon, Jean. 1992. Social class and the hidden curriculum of work. In *Rereading america: Cultural contexts for critical thinking and writing,* 521-540. Boston: St. Martins.

Anzaldúa, Gloria. 2007. *Borderlands : The new mestiza = la frontera.* 3rd ed. San Francisco: Aunt Lute Books.

Asante, Molefi. 1987. *The afrocentric idea.* Philadelphia: Temple University Press.

Bawarshi, Anis, and Stephanie Pelkowski. 2003. Postcolonialism and the idea of a writing center. In *The St. Martin's sourcebook for writing tutors,* edited by C. Murphy and S. Sherwood, 80-95. Boston: Bedford/St. Martin's.

Bean, Janet, Maryann Cucchiara, Robert Eddy, Peter Elbow, Rhonda Grego, Rich Haswell, Patricia Irvine, Eileen Kennedy, Ellie Kutz, Al Lehner, and Paul Kei Matsuda. 2006. Should we invite students to write in home languages? Complicating the yes/no debate. In *Second-language writing in the composition classroom: A critical sourcebook* edited by P. K. Matsuda, M. Cox, J. Jordan and C. Ortmeier-Hooper, New York: Bedford/St. Martin's and NCTE.

Berlin, James A. 1997. Contemporary composition: The major pedagogical theories. In *Cross-talk in comp theory: A reader,* edited by V. V. Jr., 233-248. Urbana: NCTE.

Bizzell, Patricia. 1992. *Academic discourse and critical consciousness.* Pittsburgh: University of Pittsburgh Press.

Black, Laurel Johnson. 1998. *Between talk and teaching: Reconsidering the writing conference.* Logan, Utah: Utah State University Press.

Bloom, Lynn. 1996. Freshman composition as a middle-class enterprise. *College English* 58 (6):654-675.

Boquet, Elizabeth H. 1999. 'our little secret': A history of writing centers, pre- and post-open admissions. *College Composition and Communication* 50 (3):463-482.

———. 2002. *Noise from the writing center.* Logan, Utah: Utah State University Press.

Bourdieu, Pierre. 1977. *Outline of a theory of practice.* Cambridge: Cambridge University Press.

———. 1984. *Distinction: A social critique of the judgement of taste.* Translated by R. Nice. Cambridge: Harvard University Press.

———. 1991. *Language and symbolic power.* Translated by G. Raymond and M. Adamson. Edited by J. B. Thompson. Cambridge: Harvard University Press.

Bourdieu, Pierre, and Luc J. D. Wacquant. 1992. *An invitation to reflexive sociology.* Chicago: University of Chicago Press.

Brantlinger, Patrick. 1990. *Crusoe's footprints: Cultural studies in Britain and America.* New York: Routledge.

Bruffee, Kenneth A. 1993. *Collaborative learning: Higher education, interdependence, and the authority of knowledge.* Baltimore: Johns Hopkins.

Bureau of Labor Statistics. *Education and income: More learning is key to higher earnings* 2006. Available from www.bls.gov/opub/ooq/2006/fall/oochart.pdf.

Canagarajah, A. Suresh. 2006a. The place of world englishes in composition: Pluralization continued. *College Composition & Communication* 57 (4):586-619.

———. 2006b. Understanding critical writing. In *Second-language writing in the composition classroom*, edited by P. K. Matsuda, M. Cox, J. Jordan and C. Ortmeier-Hooper, Champaign/Urbana: NCTE Press.

Cathcart, Robert S. 1983. A confrontation perspective on the study of social movements. *Central States Speech Journal* 34:69-74.

Condon, Frankie. 2007. Beyond the known: Writing centers and the work of anti-racism. *Writing Center Journal*.

Conley, Dalton. 2001. *Honky*. New York: Knoph Publishing Group.

D'Emilio, John, and Estelle Freedman. 1997. *Intimate matters: A history of sexuality in america*. 2 ed. Chicago: University of Chicago Press.

Delpit, Lisa. 1995. *Other people's children: Cultural conflict in the classroom*. New York: The New Press.

Denny, Harry. 1997a. AIDS resistance & rememberance: Mtv's tribute to and reframing of pedro zemora. *Cultural Studies: A research annual* 2:109-128.

———. 1997b. Refiguring homosexuality, "Real minorities" And civil rights: A textual analysis of colorado for family values' amendment 2 tabloid. *Cultural Studies: A research annual* 2:129-141.

———. 2005. Queering the writing center. *Writing Center Journal* 25 (2):39-62.

Dudley, Kathryn Marie. 2000. *Debt & dispossession: Farm loss in America's heartland*. Chicago: University of Chicago Press.

Duggan, Lisa. 2004. *The twilight of equality?: Neoliberalism, cultural politics, and the attack on democracy*. Boston: Beacon Press.

Ehrenreich, Barbara. 2002. *Nickle and dimed: On (not) getting by in America*. New York: Harcourt.

Elbow, Peter, and Pat Belanoff. 2003. *Being a writer: A community of writers revisited*. New York: McGraw-Hill.

Eodice, Michele. 2009. Will the rain follow the plow? WPA Conference.

Epstein, Steven. 1998. *Impure science: AIDS, activism, and the politics of knowledge*. Berkeley, CA: University of California Press.

Faigley, Lester. 1992. *Fragments of rationality: Postmodernity and the subject of composition*. Pittsburgh: University of Pittsburgh Press.

Ferris, Dana R. 2003. *Response to student writing*. Mahwah, NJ: Lawrence Erlbaum Associates.

Fitchen, Janet M. 1991. *Endangered species, enduring places: Change, identity, and survival in rural america*. Boulder, CO: Westview Press.

Flynn, Elizabeth A. 2003. Composing as a woman. In *Cross-talk in comp theory*, edited by V. Villanueva, 571-585. Champagne/Urbana, IL: NCTE Press.

Foucault, Michel. 1972. *The archeology of knowledge & the discourse on language*. New York: Pantheon.

———. 1977. *Discipline & punish: The birth of the prison*. New York: Vintage Books.

———. 1978. *The history of sexuality: An introduction, volume 1*. New York: Random House.

Fox, Thomas. 1990. *The social uses of writing: Politics and pedagogy*. Norwood: Ablex.

Fraser, Nancy. 1997. *Justice interruptus: Critical reflections on the 'postsocialist' condition*. New York: Routledge.

Freedman, Sarah Warshauer. 1984. The registers of student and professional expository writing: Influences on teachers' responses. In *New directions in composition research*, edited by R. Beach and L. S. Bridwell, 334-347. New York: Guilford.

Freire, Paulo. 2000. *Pedagogy of the oppressed*. New York: Continuum International Publishing Group.

Friedan, Betty. 1963. *The feminine mystique*. New York: W. W. Norton.

Fulkerson, Richard. 2005. Composition at the turn of the twenty first century. *College Composition and Communication* 56 (4):654-687.

Gates, Henry Louis. 1986. *"Race," Writing, and difference*. Chicago: University of Chicago Press.

Geller, Anne Ellen. 2005. Tick-tock, next: Finding epochal time in the writing center. *Writing Center Journal* 25 (1):5-4.

Geller, Anne Ellen, Michele Eodice, Frankie Condon, Meg Carroll, and Elizabeth H. Boquet. 2007. *The everyday writing center: A community of practice*. Logan, UT: Utah State University Press.

Gilyard, Keith. 1991. *Voices of the self: A study of lanugage competence*. Detroit: Wayne State University Press.

Gladwell, Malcolm. 2002. *The tipping point : How little things can make a big difference*. 1st Back Bay pbk. ed. Boston: Back Bay Books.

Goffman, Erving. 1971. *The presentation of self in everyday life*. Harmondsworth: Penguin.

———. 1974. *Stigma : Notes on the management of spoiled identity*. New York: J. Aronson.

Gramsci, Antonio. 1971. *Selections from the prison notebooks*. New York: International Publishers.

Grant, Joanne, ed. 1996. *Black protest: 350 years of history, documents,a nd analyses*. New York: Random House.

Gray-Davidson, Osha. 1996. *Broken heartland: The rise of america's rural ghetto*. Iowa City, IA: University of Iowa Press.

Grimm, Nancy. 1999. *Good intentions: Writing center work for postmodern times*. Edited by C. I. Schuster, *Cross currents: New perspectives in rhetoric and composition*. Portsmouth, NH: Heinemann.

———. 2006. Myth busting: A proposal for the public work of writing centers in fast capital times. In *National conference on writing center as public space*. University of Illinois at Chicago.

Hall, Stuart. 1993. Encoding/decoding. In *The cultural studies reader*, edited by S. During, 128-138. New York: Routledge.

Haraway, Donna. 1991. *Simians, cyborgs, and women: The reinvention of nature*. New York: Routledge.

Harl, Neil E. 1990. *Farm debt crisis of the 1980s*. Hobken, NJ: Wiley, John & Sons.

Harris, Joseph. 1997. *A teaching subject: Composition since 1966*. Upper Saddle River, NJ: Prentice Hall.

Harris, Muriel. 1986. *Teaching one-to-one: The writing conference*. Urbana: NCTE.

———. 1994. Individualized instruction in writing centers: Attending to cross-cultural differences. In *Intersections: Theory-practice in the writing center*, edited by J. A. Mullin and R. Wallace, 96-110. Urbana, IL: NCTE Press.

Harris, Muriel, and Tony Silva. 1993. Tutoring ESL students: Issues and options. *College Composition and Communication* 44 (4):525-537.

Hoggart, Richard. 1998. *The uses of literacy*. Edison, NJ: Transaction Publishers.

hooks, bell. 1989. *Talking back: Thinking feminist, thinking black*. New York: Taylor & Francis.

———. 1994. *Teaching to transgress*. New York: Oxford University Press.

Huot, Brian. 2002. *(re)articulating writing assessment for teaching and learning* Logan: Utah State University Press.

Jackson, Kenneth T. 1987. *Crabgrass frontier: The suburbanization of the u.S.* New York: Oxford University Press.

Jameson, Fredric. 1991. *Postmodernism, or, the cultural logic of late capitalism*. Durham: Duke University Press.

Jarratt, Susan C. 2001. Feminist pedagogy. In *A guide to composition pedagogies*, edited by G. Tate, A. Rupiper and K. Schick, 113-131. New York: Oxford University Press.

Kozol, Jonathan. 1992. *Savage inequalities : Children in america's schools*. 1st Harper Perennial ed. New York: HarperPerennial.

———. 2005. *The shame of the nation : The restoration of apartheid schooling in america*. New York: Crown Publishers.

Kynard, Carmen. 2007. "I want to be african": In search of a black radical tradition/african-american-vernacularized paradigm for "Students' right to their own language," Critical literacy, and "Class politics". *College English* 69 (4):360-390.

LeCourt, Donna. 2004. *Identity matters: Schooling the student body in academic discourse*. Albany, NY: State University of New York Press.

———. 2006. Performing working-class identity in composition: Toward a pedagogy of textual practice. *College English* 69 (1).

Leki, Ilona. 1992. *Understanding ESL writers: A guide for teachers*. Portsmouth, NH: Boynton/Cook Publishers.

Lemann, Nicholas. 1992. *The promised land : The great black migration and how it changed america*. 1st Vintage Books ed. New York: Vintage Books.

Lindquist, Julie. 2002. *A place to stand: Politics and puersuasion in a working-class bar*. New York: Oxford University Press.

Liu, Eric. 1999. *The accidental asian: Notes of a native son*. New York: Random House.

Logue, Cal M. 1981. Transcending coercion: The communicative strategies of black slaves on antebellum plantations. *Quarterly Journal of Speech* 67:31-46.

Lu, Min-Zhan. 1994. Professing multiculturalism: The politics of style in the contact zone. *College Composition and Communication* 45:305-321.

Lunsford, Andrea. 1991. Collaboration, control, and the idea of a writing center. In *Landmark essays on writing centers*, edited by C. Murphy and J. Law, 109-116. Davis, CA: Hermagoras Press.

Lutes, Jean Marie. 2002. Why feminists make better tutors: Gender and disciplinary expertise in a curriculum-based tutoring program. In *Writing center research: Extending the conversation*, edited by P. Gillespie, A. Gillam, L. F. Brown and B. Stay, 235-257. Mahwah, NJ: Lawrence Erlbaum Associates.

Matsuda, Paul. 2004. Facing ESL writers in the writing centers. In *Northeast Writing Centers Association*. Merrimack College, North Andover, MA.

Matsuda, Paul Kei. 2003. Composition studies and ESL writing: A disciplinary division of labor. In *Cross-talk in comp theory*, edited by V. Villanueva, 773-796. Urbana, IL: NCTE Press.

———. 2006. Second-language writing in the twentieth century: A situated historical perspective. In *Second-language writing the composition classroom*, edited by P. K. Matsuda, M. Cox, J. Jordan and C. Ortmeier-Hooper, 14-30. Champaign/Urbana: NCTE Press.

McBride, James. 2006. *The color of water: A black man's tribute to his white mother*. New York: Penguin.

Meyer, Emily, and Louise Z. Smith. 1987. *The practical tutor*. New York: Oxford University Press.

Miller, Richard. 2005. *Writing at the end of the world*. Pittsburgh: University of Pittsburgh Press.

Miller, Susan. 1991. The feminization of composition. In *The politics of writing instruction: Postsecondary*, edited by C. Schuster, 39-53. Portsmouth, NH: Boyton/Cook Publishers.

North, Stephen M. 1984/1995. The idea of a writing center. In *Landmark essays on writing centers*, edited by C. Murphy and J. Law, 71-86. Davis, CA: Hermagoras Press.

Omi, Michael, and Howard Winant. 1986. *Racial formation in the united states: From the 1960s to the 1980s*. New York: Routledge.

Owens, Derek. 2008. Hideaways and hangouts, public squares and performance sites: New metaphors for writing center design. In *Creative approaches to writing center work*, edited by S. Bruce and K. Dvorak, 70-84. Cresskill, NJ: Hampton Press.

Parks, Stephen. 1999. *Class politics: The movement for the student's right to their own language.* Urbana: NCTE Press.

Patton, Cindy. 1985. *Sex and germs: The politics of AIDS*. Boston: South End Press.

———. 1990. *Inventing AIDS*. New York: Routledge.

———. 1995. Refiguring social space. In *Social postmodernism: Beyond identity politics*, edited by S. Seidman and L. Nicholson, 216-249. Cambridge: Cambridge University Press.

———. 2002. *Globalizing AIDS*. Minneapolis: University of Minnesota Press.

Patton, Cindy, and Robert L. Caserio. 2000. Introduction, citizenship 2000. *Cultural Studies* 14 (1):1-14.

Paula Gillespie, Bradley Hughes, Harvey Kail. 2007. Nothing marginal about this writing center experience: Using research about peer tutor alumni to educate others, edited by J. William J. Macauley and N. Mauriello, Cresskill, NJ: Hampton Press.

Pennycook, Alastair. 2007. *Global englishes and transcultural flows*. New York: Routledge.

Reid, Joy. 2006. "Eye" Learners and "Ear" Learners: Identifying the language needs of international student and u.S. Resident writers In *Second-language writing in the composition classroom*, edited by P. Matsuda, M. Cox, J. Jordan and C. Ortmeier, New York: Bedford/St. Martin's.

Rodriguez, Richard. 1983. *Hunger of memory: The education of richard rodriguez*. New York: Bantam Doubleday Dell Publishing.

Rose, Mike. 2005. *Lives on the boundary*. New York: Viking Penguin.

Royster, Jacqueline Jones. 1996. When the first voice you hear is not your own. *College Composition & Communication* 47 (1):29-40.

Sedgwick, Eve Kosofsky. 1990. *Epistemology of the closet*. Berkeley, CA: University of California Press.

Severino, Carol. 2004. Avoiding appropriation. In *ESL writers: A guide for writing center tutors*, edited by S. Bruce and B. Rafoth, 48-59. Boston: Boynton/Cook.

———. 2006. The sociopolitical implications of response to second-language and second-dialect writing. In *Second-language writing in the composition classroom*, edited by P. K. Matsuda, M. Cox, J. Jordan and C. Ortmeier-Hooper, 333-350. Champaign/Urbana: NCTE Press.

Shaughnessy, Mina P. 1977. *Errors & expectations: A guide for the teacher of basic writing*. New York: Oxford University Press.

———. 1997. Diving in: An introduction to basic writing. In *Cross-talk in comp theory: A reader*, edited by V. Villanueva, 289-296. Urbana: NCTE.

Shor, Ira. 1992. *Empowering education : Critical teaching for social change*. Chicago: University of Chicago Press.

Silva, Tony, and Paul Kei Matsuda, eds. 2001. *On second language writing*. Mahwah, NJ: Lawrence Erlbaum Associates, Publishers.

Smitherman, Geneva. 1977. *Talkin and testifyin*. Detroit: Wayne State University Press.

Sontag, Susan. 1989. *AIDS and its metaphors*. 1st ed. New York: Farrar, Straus and Giroux.

———. 1990. *Illness as metaphor ; and, AIDS and its metaphors*. 1st Anchor Books ed. New York: Doubleday.

Swales, John. 1987. Approaching the concept of discourse community. In *Conference on College Composition and Communication*. Atlanta, GA.

Villanueva, Victor. 1993. *Bootstraps: From an american academic of color*. Urbana, IL: NCTE.

———. 2003. On the rhetoric and precedents of racism. In *Cross-talk in comp theory: A reader*, edited by V. Villanueva, 829-845. Urbana, IL: NCTE. Original edition, College Composition and Communication 50.4: 645-61.

————. 2006. Blind: Talking about the new racism. *Writing Center Journal* 26 (1):3-19.

Welch, Nancy. 1999. Playing with reality: Writing centers after the mirror stage. *College compositions and communication* 51 (1):51-69.

Wenger, Etienne. 1998. *Communities of practice: Learning, meaning, and identity.* Cambridge: Cambridge University Press.

Williams, Raymond. 1983. *Culture & society.* New York: Columbia University Press.

Willis, Paul. 1981. *Learning to labor: How working class kids get working class jobs.* New York: Columbia University Press.

Woolbright, Meg. 2003. The politics of tutoring: Feminism within the patriarchy. In *The st. Martin's sourcebook for writing tutors,* edited by C. Murphy and S. Sherwood, 67-80. Boston: Bedford/St. Martin's.

X, Malcolm. 1965. *Malcolm X speaks.* New York: Merit Publishers.

Yoshino, Kenji. 2007. *Covering: The hidden assault on american civil rights.* New York: Random House.

INDEX

ABOUT THE AUTHOR

HARRY DENNY is an assistant professor of English at St. John's University in New York City. Through its Institute for Writing Studies, he directs writing centers on its Queens and Staten Island campuses and does research on composition and writing center studies, cultural studies and social justice. Denny is active in writing center community organizing and leadership in the New York City, the Northeast Writing Centers Association, and the International Writing Centers Association. He is currently at work on projects that focus on research methods for writing centers as well as critical explorations of space and the negotiation of professional identities in the field.